Smile...

There's a well-known saying that the best camera for any job isn't necessarily the most expensive, the most powerful or the one with the broadest set of features. It's the one you happen to have on your person when the opportunity presents itself.

In almost every instance, then, the best camera today is the one that forms part of your smartphone. It's almost certainly in your pocket or bag when you leave the house, and when you get back home it's sitting on the kitchen counter, or perched on the arm of your chair. We live our lives with our phones – and our cameras – and as a result we're taking more pictures than at any previous time in the history of our species.

If you're lucky enough to own a recent iPhone, you're in an enviable position. Not only do you have a great phone for day to day use, but you also have access to a five- or eight-megapixel camera, an easy way to share your photos online courtesy of the built-in social networking tools, and an enviable collection of third-party image editing applications to choose from.

With an iPhone by your side, you have a complete portable darkroom in one tiny tablet, with more power than even a top-end desktop computer would have boasted a few years ago.

It's easy to quickly squeeze off a few shots, but a bit of care, consideration and forethought will immesurably improve your results.

So will downloading a handful of editing apps and – depending on your budget – buying some add-on lenses.

In this guide, then, we'll focus on the iPhone 4, 4S and 5, and show you how you can enhance your smartphone photography, both by improving your technique and by kitting yourself out with the best tools for the job.

It isn't expensive and it isn't difficult, but it certainly is a whole lot of fun.

— *Nik Rawlinson*

The world of iPhone photography

Photo Stream

Complete Guide to iPhone Photography

WRITTEN BY Nik Rawlinson

ADVERTISING
MAGBOOK ACCOUNT MANAGER • Katie Wood • 07971 937162
DIGITAL PRODUCTION MANAGER • Nicky Baker • 020 8907 6056

DENNIS PUBLISHING LTD
GROUP MANAGING DIRECTOR • Ian Westwood
MANAGING DIRECTOR • John Garewal
MD OF ADVERTISING • Julian Lloyd-Evans
NEWSTRADE DIRECTOR • David Barker
CHIEF OPERATING OFFICER • Brett Reynolds
GROUP FINANCE DIRECTOR • Ian Leggett
CHIEF EXECUTIVE • James Tye
CHAIRMAN • Felix Dennis

PUBLISHING AND MARKETING
MAGBOOK PUBLISHER • Dharmesh Mistry • 020 7907 6100
MARKETING EXECUTIVE • Paul Goodhead • 020 7907 6012

You don't make a photograph just
with a camera. You bring to the
act of photography all the pictures
you have seen, the books you have
read, the music you have heard, the
people you have loved.

Ansel Adams
landscape photographer

 Click. Boom. Amazing!

Steve Jobs
co-inventor of the iPhone

Chapter 1
An iPhone for photography

The best iPhone for photography

The iPhone 5 may – at the time of writing – be the latest and greatest phone to emerge from Apple's labs, and it's certainly the most exciting, but just as it did when it released the iPhone 4 and iPhone 4S, Apple hasn't immediately retired its predecessors. The prime reason for doing so is that it allows network providers to sign up new customers with cheaper handsets who might otherwise be put off by the cost of the latest upgrade.

This is good news for the iPhone photographer as it means you can take part in this exciting hobby without having to pay quite so much as you might have expected.

It's fair to say that the camera on the very first iPhone was rather underwhelming. It had a resolution of only two megapixels and the image

Over successive generations, the iPhone's rear camera has improved to an extraordinary degree, and since the iPhone 4 it has been supplemented by a FaceTime camera to the front.

quality wasn't that great. Over the years, though, Apple has done much to improve things and now the iPhone sports one of the best cameras you'll find in any smartphone device. In fact, since Apple shipped the iPhone 4, every device has included not one but two cameras. The one in the back of the case is the higher resolution device that we'll use to shoot photographs throughout this book, and the one in the front – beside the earpiece – is a lower resolution sensor used primarily for video conferencing with Apple's own FaceTime software or third-party alternatives like Skype.

So, with a set budget in mind, how do you choose the best iPhone for you?

iPhone 4 and iPhone 4S

The iPhone 4 is knocking on a bit now, but it shouldn't be discounted out of hand. It can run iOS 6, which at the time of writing is the latest release of Apple's mobile operating system for the iPhone, iPad and iPod touch.

It boasts the same Retina Display as the iPhone 4S, but although the pixel density is the same as it is on the iPhone 5, which means the image quality is identical, the screen is smaller. In both the iPhone 4S and iPhone 4, the screen measures only 3.5 inches from corner to corner, and its overall resolution is 960×640 pixels.

Whenever it ships a new iPhone, Apple retains the previous model. At the time of writing, the iPhone 4S (above) and iPhone 4 remained on sale alongside iPhone 5.

Before this puts you off, though, consider the fact that this is a much higher resolution than a regular computer display would have been five or 10 years ago, yet we wouldn't have balked at the idea of editing our images on a screen that size back then. So, why not do the same with your iPhone?

What really sets apart the iPhone 4 and iPhone 4S is the processor. Inside the iPhone 4 it is an Apple designed A4 chip. In the iPhone 4S, you'll find the A5 chip. As its name would suggest, the A5 is faster and more up-to-date, and you'll notice this when launching the camera application, taking photos and performing edits. So, if your budget doesn't stretch to an iPhone 5 at least see if you can nab an iPhone 4S, even if it means saving up a little longer, as you'll find the photographic experience much more rewarding.

However, there's a more important consideration where portable photography is concerned, and that's resolution. The back camera in the iPhone 4 has just a 5 megapixel sensor, and so produces images that are 2592×1936 pixels. That's still quite a lot, and online photo printing services would be happy to receive images as small as 4 megapixels – smaller than those produced by the iPhone 4 – when printing A2-sized canvases and posters.

The iPhone 4S, however, has an 8 megapixel sensor and so produces images that are 3264×2448 pixels. So, if printing services are happy to produce such large products from images smaller than those captured by an iPhone 4, is it really worth the extra expense to buy the 4S if you aren't so bothered about the speed improvements delivered by the fast processor?

Almost certainly, the answer is still 'yes'. If you start with a larger image, you can crop it more tightly to change the composition in post-production while retaining a high enough number of pixels in the finished product to still print at large sizes. If, on the other hand, you started with the 5 megapixel images produced by the iPhone 4 rather than the 8 megapixel images produced by the iPhone 4S, cropping it so that the same subject dominates the frame

Every current iPhone has the ability to shoot video as well as still images using both the high resolution back- and lower resolution front-mounted cameras.

might leave you with too few pixels to play with when it comes to printing.

So, from a technical standpoint the iPhone 4S is better in both aspects: it's faster and it produces higher resolution images. However, from a purely artistic standpoint there is another reason to recommend the iPhone 4S over and above the iPhone 4.

The camera mechanism on the iPhone 4 has a fixed aperture of f/2.8; and the iPhone 4S, it's f/2.4. What does this mean? Well, regardless of what you use to take your photos, the aperture determines the depth of field, or the distance between the closest and furthest objects in your image that remain in focus. The wider the aperture, the shallower the depth of field, and so the more easily you can isolate portrait subjects against a defocussed background for a very appealing result.

At f/2.4, the maximum aperture of the iPhone 4S is wider than that of the iPhone 4, and so not only will it let in more light, thus enabling shorter exposures which will in turn reduce the likelihood that any shaking on the part of your hands – however minor – will blur the image, but it will also produce better portraits and macro (close-up) shots.

If you will predominantly be shooting landscapes and general scenic views, then this will naturally be of less interest, although the hybrid infrared filter on the iPhone 4S and 5 lens will likely be more

tempting. So, too, will be the ability to shoot panoramas in-camera using the new panorama feature in iOS 6. Although the iPhone 4 can be upgraded to run iOS 6, and new handsets will ship with iOS 6 already installed, the panorama feature only works on the iPhone 4S and iPhone 5.

iPhone 5

Like the iPhone 4S, the iPhone 5 has an 8 megapixel sensor putting out images that are 3264×2448 pixels each. These obviously afford the same cropping options as those produced by the iPhone 4S. It has the same five element lens, face detection, infrared filter and f/2.4 aperture as the 4S, each of which is missing from the iPhone 4.

That begs the question, why would you pay the extra for an iPhone 5 when you could get pretty much the same features with the iPhone 4S? In all honesty, if you are doing a cold financial analysis, the answer would be that you wouldn't.

However, the iPhone 5 sports Apple's latest processor – the A6 chip – which is up to twice as fast as the A5 in the iPhone 4S, and in particular boosts graphics performance. So, the iPhone's native photo app, and those from third-party coders, will launch more quickly so you'll have a better chance of snapping a spontaneous event. Then, once you come to edit your images, you should find your editing tool of choice to be snappier and more responsive. For the serious smartphone photographer, then, the iPhone 5 makes sense.

The higher resolution display, which is now 4in from corner to corner rather than just 3.5in, sports the same at 640 pixels across but is now 1136 pixels tall. Naturally, when held in landscape orientation, this helps enormously when you're reviewing or editing panoramas shot using iOS 6. Despite this, the iPhone 5 is just 9 mm taller than the iPhone 4 and iPhone 4S, it's the same width and it's actually a little slimmer from front to back.

The best iPhone for videography

Although videography isn't within the remit of this book, it's worth considering for a moment the differences between the various current iPhone models when it comes to shooting movies. Here, again, the iPhone 5 wins hands down.

The iPhone 4 can shoot 720p video at 30 frames per second using the rear camera. It can use the LED light to illuminate the scene and lets you tap the screen to refocus while filming. That's not bad for a phone.

The iPhone 4S builds upon this by adding in video stabilisation, and the iPhone 5 takes things further still. Apple claims that the video stabilisation is

more effective on the iPhone 5 than on either previous device, it can employ the same face detection features as it does when shooting stills, and you can now shoot still photos while recording video, all the while shooting movies at 1080p – a considerably higher resolution than that supported by the iPhone 4.

Around the front, the camera set into the face of the iPhone beside the earpiece on the iPhone 4 and 4S can shoot VGA resolution (640×480) stills and video, but on the iPhone 5 it has been upgraded so that it can shoot 1.2 megapixel stills (1280×960) and 720p video.

Even in the video realm, then, the iPhone 5 looks the better bet.

The best iPhone for photography

So which is the best iPhone for taking photos? Quite obviously it's the iPhone 5, And so it should be, as it's the most expensive iPhone on the market.

However, if your budget doesn't stretch that far there's no reason why you should have to overextend yourself. The iPhone 4S boasts almost identical specs where the camera is concerned, and produces images of the same size. It can also shoot panoramas when using iOS 6.

If you're buying a phone primarily to use for making calls, sending texts, and taking photos, then there really is very little to choose between the iPhone 4S and iPhone 5. The main difference will likely be a minor speed decrease on downgrading to the 4S.

Does that mean the iPhone 4 is out of the question? Absolutely not. Its camera might only produce images of 5 megapixels, it's missing the panorama and face detection features, it doesn't have the hybrid infrared filter of the iPhone 4S and iPhone 5, and the lens aperture may be slightly narrower, but it remains a great phone for taking photos,

and everything covered in this guide apart from the native panorama feature should work just as well on this device as on the later two models.

Perhaps the most sensible reason to opt for the iPhone 4 rather than the latest, greatest upgrades, though, is that on many contracts you can now pick one up for free, and so if you're going to be paying a monthly fee for your cellphone anyhow, why not bag an iPhone and enjoy the photo-shooting opportunities it affords?

	iPhone 5	iPhone 4S	iPhone 4
Processor	A6	A5	A4
Resolution	8 megapixels	8 megapixels	5 megapixels
Aperture	f/2.4	f/2.4	f/2.8
Autofocus	Yes	Yes	Yes
Tap to focus	Yes	Yes	Yes
LED flash	Yes	Yes	Yes
BSI sensor	Yes	Yes	Yes
Lens elements	5	5	4
Face detection	Yes	Yes	No
Hybrid IR filter	Yes	Yes	No
Panorama mode	Yes	Yes	No
Movie resolution	1080p 30fps	1080p 30fps	720p 30fps
Front resolution	1.2 megapixels	640 x 480	640 x 480

Chapter 2
Technique

iPhone photography conventions

If you've just bought your first iPhone and you're about to launch into the world of smartphone photography, it's important to make sure you're familiar with the general conventions that govern how you work with, use and control your device – particularly when using the default camera app.

Tap to focus

You'll already know that you can tap to select objects in the regular iOS interface. Tapping in the same way in the camera app selects the point of focus in your photo and simultaneously sets the exposure with reference to that point. If that point is much darker than its surroundings, the overall brightness will be increased and those surroundings may be bleached out, so be careful to compose balanced shots wherever possible (see the spread on Camera Awesome, pp42 - 43, which can help overcome this issue).

Unpinch to zoom

Further, while tapping in this way brings up a slider that lets you zoom in and out, you can save time by placing two fingers together on the screen and moving them apart from one another – unpincing – in the same way you might in the Maps app when you want to zoom in

Tapping the screen and then dragging the slider lets you zoom in and out, but you can achieve the same in less time – and often with greater accuracy – by simply pinching and unpinching the scene directly.

on the map. In the camera application, this has an equivalent effect, zooming in on your framed scene. This saves time by cutting out the slider and often produces more accurate framing.

There are two cameras on the iPhone, and you can switch between them by tapping the icon of the curved arrows icon at the top of the screen. This lets you take pictures of yourself while seeing what you look like in the display, although at a lower resolution than you would if you stuck with the rear camera.

However, shooting with the rear camera to take the highest resolution self-portraits isn't without issues, and introduces an extra complication in that you won't be able to see the on-screen shutter button. So, you may have to tap around the screen a couple of times until you hit it.

You might think that headphones are only good for one thing: listening to your iTunes. However, with Apple having implemented a handy press to shoot feature on the iPhone's volume up control you can also use the bundled headphones as a handy remote shutter release.

Unfortunately this will simultaneously change the point of focus and the spot used to gauge the correct exposure, so you could end up with an incorrectly framed or unevenly lit result.

Click to shoot

There is a solution, however, which is to use the physical volume up button on the side of the iPhone body to fire the shutter release.

This still isn't perfect, as the result could end up being a picture of you holding out your iPhone art arm's length, which is a bit of a cliché. Fortunately, taking a picture this way relies less on pressing that specific button, and more on simply increasing the volume.

So, plug in a pair of earphones with a built-in volume control (the ones that shipped with your iPhone are perfect in this respect) and press the '+' button on these instead. You'll still fire the shutter, but this time around you won't also snap a picture of your looming arm, as you should have sufficient slack to keep your hands in a more neutral position.

iPhone photography principles

You might not see how, but your iPhone has a lot more in common with a regular camera than you might think. If you ignore all of the telephone, internet communications and supplementary apps, and just focus on the camera, you'll find that a lot of the rules of conventional photography apply here, too, as we'll show you in this section.

The rule of thirds

Perhaps the most important rule in the whole of photography, the rule of thirds, is the first you should learn, and the one you should remember even if you forget everything else, as it's the key to producing more powerful and visually pleasing results.

To put it in the most succinct way possible, imagine that every frame you shoot is divided into three, both vertically and horizontally, giving you nine squares and four points at which they intersect. The result will look very similar to a noughts and crosses (tic tac toe) board, like this:

The secret to effective and powerful photography is to align important elements of your image either with the lines or – even better – with the points at which they intersect and, if you're shooting portraits, to have your subjects either looking towards the camera or away from the edge.

So, if your subject was a person and were to line them up with the left-hand vertical line you have them either facing the camera directly, or looking to the right. If they were positioned on the right-hand vertical line, you would have them looking forwards or left through the frame.

If you're taking a close-up shot of someone's face you would generally try and line up their eyes with the upper horizontal line passing through the frame a third of the way down from the top. If you were taking a longer body shot then it would be more appropriate to position their face on the line. For the very best results you would combine both theories so that their body was running down one of the vertical lines and their face was on a horizontal intersection.

With two horizontal and two vertical divisions in the frame you have a total of nine boxes and four intersections within your image

Theory: Rule of thirds in practice

Roughly one third of the width is occupied by the man, one third by the baby and one third by the space between their faces

This eye is aligned with one of the vertical divisions in the image

These eyes appear on one of the one-third lines, and so are powerful in the image

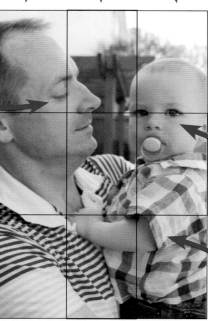

The baby's arm appears just below one of the power lines in the image and therefore appears to emphasise the effect. The hand is right on the line itself.

The iPhone's native camera application makes it very easy to work with the rule of thirds as it includes a built-in set of guidelines for use when shooting stills. To enable the guides, tap Options and then tap the slider beside Grid so that it reads ON. Tap Done when you have finished setting your options.

As with all rules, though, the rule of thirds should only be observed when it works for the particular shot you are taking. Sometimes it pays to break the rules, as can be seen in the image below, which puts the point of focus – a reflected corner of the glass pyramid at the centre of the Louvre, in the very centre of the frame.

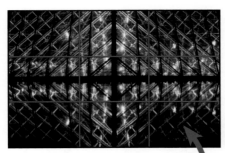

In this instance, aligning the corner of the pyramid with one of the one-third power lines in the frame would have resulted in a less powerful composition. This photo only works because the elements are perfectly balanced in the very centre of the frame.

Technique: Rule of Thirds

You can play around with the rule of thirds to create different results. In the image above we have placed both the nose and the eye on the left hand line, and the mouth on the right. It doesn't matter that we are breaking one of our later rules to keep the eyes in focus as the overall result remains a pleasant composition. Likewise, in the frame below the first third of the image contains a focused Q, with the focus falling off through the remaining part.

The image above again makes good use of the rule of thirds to direct the composition. The main subject is the drum, which the man is warming by the fire before he starts to play. However, the fire is the most obvious elements as it is the brighest part of the image, and the man is the most interesting element, as we always identify with other humans. Aligning these two elements with the vertical lines set a third of the way into the image therefore make the photo stronger, even if the drum no longer becomes the point on which we focus first.

Only one of the lines in our grid is aligned with an element in the image to the right. However, it is one of the strongest and most clearly-defined elements of the whole frame, where two walls in this narrow Lyon courtyard approach one another, effectively drawing the right-hand line themselves.

Technique: Optimising exposure and focus

Original image

HDR-optimised image

Above: Even if you can't get the perfect exposure by tapping on the subject of your image, which would have been impossible in this long-focus shot of a loch at sunset, you can set the iPhone to optimise your results by applying its HDR processing algorythms. These examine the highlights and shadows in your image and tweak them so that the maximum possible level of information can be extracted from the frame you have captured. The result, as can be seen above, is that the image on the right, to which HDR processing has been applied, is slightly more saturated, and the clouds are clearer, than they are in the unprocessed image on the left.

As well as balancing out the overall tones in an image, as we saw with the sunset example above, the HDR feature does a very good job of lightening up specific parts of a photo, such as the child's face seen here, without affecting parts that are already accurately exposed, like the magazine cover behind which he's hiding.

HDR is an extremely versatile tool, and one that you just need to turn on and forget. In many situations it can preserve detail that would otherwise be lost, as we can see here in this shot of Liege station, Belgium. It was taken in a rush through a train window, and as is evident from the top image, failing to take time to properly set the exposure has resulted in a burned-out roof, lacking detail. In the lower frame, HDR has preserved the roof detail entirely.

Set focus and exposure

On a regular digital camera, you half-press the shutter release to lock the focus and exposure before going on to depress it fully to fire the shutter.

You can't have failed to notice that this feature is missing from the iPhone. It doesn't have a conventional button – unless you count the shutter function of the volume control – and most of the pictures you take will be fired by tapping a button on the screen.

However, that's not to say that you can't emulate the half-pressed shutter trick on the iPhone; you just have to think in a more conventional multitouch manner and plan ahead slightly.

It works like this. Frame your image in the usual way and then tap the screen on the main subject of your shot. This will tell the Camera app that this is the element it must pay most attention to when setting the brightness, contrast and focus of your shot.

You will notice that the image bounces briefly as the iPhone checks that it has got the best possible fix on the subject for sharp focus, and the colours and light level on the screen will likely fluctuate as it compensates for the specific requirements of that part of the image. When you then take the picture in the conventional manner by tapping the on-screen button, the result will be a better-exposed and clearer image.

Know when to use the flash

Your iPhone has a built in flash, which naturally enough is used to illuminate darker scenes.

However, as you'll see from the Technique box to the right there are several instances when it would be inappropriate to use it, and we're not just talking about those occasions on which it would be rude.

Remember that the flash has a limited range and it won't be able to illuminate everything in a scene if you are taking a landscape shot. In an instance such as that you're likely to find that activating the flash only serves to force your iPhone to select a faster shutter speed, which will result in less light reaching the sensor, and an even darker result than you would have achieved without the flash.

Likewise, be careful about using the flash when you're standing particularly close to your subject. As a bright light source, the flash is prone to bouncing off skin and the backs of peoples' eyes, the latter of which results in the infamous red eye effect.

Finally, don't forget that there are many times when the flash is useful in bright sunlight. If the light source is positioned behind your subject it will appear in silhouette. Forcing your iPhone to use its flash in such an instance will accurate expose them.

Technique: Using the flash

For the sake of speed and simplicity, you'll want to keep the flash turned off most of the time. On the whole, you'll rarely need to use it as the iPhone will compensate in other ways for scenes shot in low light.

However, there are some occasions when you could do with boosting the illumination in your shots, and that's when the flash should be put to good use. For example, as in the example here, when shooting a backlit subject such as this flower head, forcing the flash to fire can pay dividends as it will illuminate the front of the flower head, which would otherwise be cast into shadow by the strong rear illumination.

In instances such as this, tap the flash button in the top left corner of the camera app interface and set it to ON. Setting it to Auto won't work in this situation as the iPhone will consider there to be sufficient light in the scene already as it gauges the background.

This flower was shot against a bright sky, with the sun positioned directly behind the petals. Naturally, this achieved the effect we were after on the stem of the plant on the image to the left, as it highlighted the hairs and fibres by illuminating them. However, it has done nothing for the head of the plant, which has been thrown into a stark silhouette which thus lacks detail in the captured image. Had we used the flash we would have been able to illuminate the petals on the side facing the camera and revealed far more detail in the finished photo, leaving us with a shot more like the image on the right, which is better balanced and more satisfying overall.

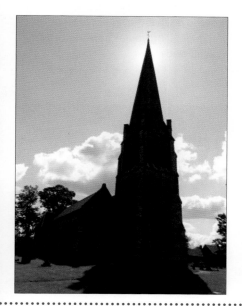

There are some situations when using the flash will have no visible effect at all. A prime example is when shooting larger objects that are backlit, such as the church to the left.

Although this is a striking image because of the way that the shadow looms towards the lens, the grass between the camera and the church, and the actual illumination of the tower itself, are severely compromised by the strong backlighting from the sun.

Unless you specifically want to achieve the effect seen here, where the subject is silhouetted, the only way to fix this problem without using large quantities of industrial lights is to recompose the shot entirely.

Shooting people

Portraits are among the most common subjects shot with a smartphone camera. If you carry a phone in your pocket, you'll always have a camera with you, so it's easy to whip it out at a moment's notice and capture a spontaneous moment.

The key to shooting successful portraits is to keep your subjects' eyes in focus even if the rest of the picture is out of focus. Because, as humans, we engage with the eyes in the picture first, sharp eyes make for a stiking picture and help excuse any other mistake you may have made in your composition.

Have your subject either look directly at the camera, or well away from it. Don't let them look just off to one side, or your viewer will wonder what it is they're finding so interesting just outside of the frame.

When shooting children, try and involve their parents in the shot wherever possible, as it will keep them calm. Engage them in the photo-making process so that they react to where you're pointing your iPhone, rather than looking elsewhere.

Shooting animals

It can be very difficult to accurately frame an animal and have them stay where you put them, so unless they're particularly well trained you'll have to largely work around their own whims.

It can help to shoot from a slight distance, though, or to have someone else keep them entertained while you get them in the frame. Also, turn off the flash or the constant iPhone illumination option so that you reduce the chances of distracting them.

Landscape photography

The key in landscape photography is to either keep your horizon perfectly level or to skew it to such a degree that it's obvious you never wanted it aligned in the first place. Check out Camera Awesome, pp42 - 43, which can help here thanks to its built in level guide.

However, there's no reason why landscape photography has to take a broad view of the scene in front of you; it could just as easily be a representation of what is above or below you, so shift your position to capture details of the world around you.

If you're serious about shooting this kind of subject then see if your budget will stretch to a more up to date iPhone or, if you already have an iPhone 4S, make sure you're running at least iOS 6 so you can take advantage of the new built-in panorama feature. Just bear in mind that this doesn't also apply the HDR filter.

Sporting events

Shooting sports is asking rather a lot of the iPhone in its default condition. However, adding on an external lens that offers telephoto capabilities will help get you closer to the action.

At the same time, choosing a different photography application to the default camera app that's bundled as part of iOS will enable you to shoot high speed bursts so you have more chance of capturing a winning moment. Just be wary of the fact that very high speed bust modes can usually only achieve such high speeds because they cut the resolution of the picture.

Don't worry if you don't have either an external lens or an app, though, as there are still plenty of opportunities for inventive photos. Why not snap your fellow fans, as we have above?

Shooting panoramas in iOS 6

iOS 6, the most recent update to Apple's operating system for the iPhone, iPod touch and iPad, introduced a new feature for users of the iPhone 5 and iPhone 4S: panorama photography. Sadly it's not available in the iPhone 4 and earlier, perhaps because their processors don't have the necessary speed and power to process the incoming data or – more likely – because it would both reward those users who have recently upgraded, and possibly encourage an upgrade from users of earlier models.

It's not something we haven't seen on the iPhone before – there have been plenty of third-party panorama apps – but its appearance in iOS 6 marks the first time Apple has provided panorama features itself.

The panorama function is hidden behind the options button at the top of the screen, just like the HDR switch and the option to use grid lines to help you keep various picture elements on the four power points in the frame.

Once activated, it allows you to set your start point before you tap the regular shutter button and start panning across the scene in front of you. If you move too slowly or too quickly it won't work, so use a steady pace and watch the preview bar fill up. Once you get to the end, it saves the image or, if you want to stop before you get there, tap *DONE* to close off the panorama.

Technique: Shooting panoramas

[1] Open the camera options by tapping the Options button at the top of the screen. Here you'll find the HDR and grid controls that were also present in iOS 5 and earlier, plus the new Panorama button. There are no tweaks to apply; simply tap it and follow the instructions.

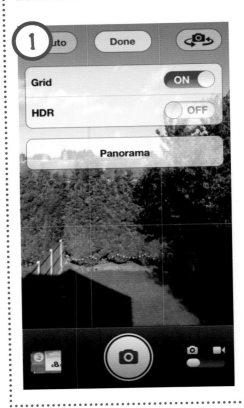

[2] Panorama isn't active right away. As with taking a regular photo, you need to tap the shutter button at the bottom of the screen to get started. So, frame the starting point of your panorama, which should be to the left of the sweep, and wait a second for it to set the exposure and focus, then tap to begin.

[3] Sweep your iPhone across the scene in the direction indicated by the arrow, and watch as the app builds up the panorama in real time across the centre of the display. It will automatically stop when the preview bar is full, but if you don't want to take such a wide sweep, tap DONE when you want to stop.

Tall panoramas

At first it would appear that the panorama function only works from left to right, and that's true, but there's nothing to stop you from tipping your iPhone on one side and panning up or down to capture a portrait-orientation panorama for taller pictures (*left*).

This can introduce complications where exposure is concerned, though, since it will often mean that you are panning from a dark landscape to a bright sky or vice-versa. Starting from the landscape and panning upwards can result in a bleached-out sky, while starting with the sky will often give you a satisfying blue starting point, and a landscape that's entirely lost in the shadows.

The panorama feature lets you take pictures that encompass a sweep of up to 240 degrees around your current position. The result, as can be seen above, is a much wider representation of your location. Compare it to the regular shot, to the left, which captures only the central portion.

The smaller frame to the left has greater impact because rather than being extracted from a panorama it was shot as a stand-alone photo, which means it benefits from the iPhone's built-in HDR processing.

Managing camera settings

Apple centralises the settings for all of the iPhone's core applications – including the camera – in a unified Settings application. In the iPhone's default state you'll find this on the first home screen (see icon, above right).

The camera settings are bundled up with those for the Photos application in Photos & Camera.

Most of the settings you'll find here – which we've outlined on the opposite page – deal with the way that your photos are played back, synchronised or shared with friends.

However, one setting here has a direct affect on your images at the point at which you shoot them: whether or not it should keep the 'normal' photo when creating a high dynamic range version.

High dynamic range (HDR) photos usually have a higher amount of detail than regular shots as the iPhone looks to balance the tones and different levels of illumination in the picture so that there are no burned-out areas or shadows so deep that their contents are rendered close to black.

However, to do this your iPhone will have to make some fundamental changes to the image, which may 'improve' the result to such a degree that it doesn't reflect the original scene any more. In these instances you will want to step back to the image's native state so that you can either enjoy the more accurate representation of the image you were hoping for, or apply your own edits in a regular photo editor.

Like all the best rules, there are a few exceptions here, and Apple has hived off a few settings to the Camera and Photos applications themselves.

In the Camera application, the Options button at the top of the screen lets you enable the grid lines that we discussed in the general photography principles pages at the start of this section, and the HDR feature itself. Elsewhere on the top line you'll also find the option to turn on the flash and an icon showing a camera with two curved arrows below it. Tapping this switches between the front and back cameras.

In the Photos application, you have only one set of options, which reveal themselves when you start to play back a slideshow. As you can see from the grab below, these let you set the transition style used to move between images, and specify whether or not it should simultaneously play music selected from your iPhone library.

iPhone Camera settings

If you have an iCloud account, be sure to enable My Photo Stream so that your images are automatically synchronised to your other devices, and Mac or PC, by way of Apple's servers. It's free!

Shared Photo Streams allow you to publish your photos online so that you don't need to email them or post to a social network. Again, it's a free component of iCloud. Once published you can email a direct link to your shared stream to friends.

Slideshows let you set the iPhone to step through your photos one at a time, displaying them on the screen so that you don't need to manually slide from one to another. These are only half of the slideshow settings, though, as tapping Play on a library of thumbnails to start the slideshow going will first present you with supplementary options for simultaneously playing music and selecting a transition style.

When the Camera app creates an HDR version of your image to maximise the amount of detail it shows, it needs to make adjustments. It's wise to also keep a copy of the original should you ever need it.

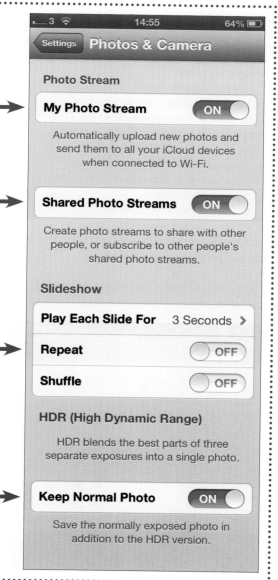

35

Managing camera location settings

One of the primary benefits of using a phone as your camera is that you will always know where any one of your images was shot.

Phones like the iPhone, and most of its up-to-date rivals, feature a built-in GPS receiver. This supplements the data that it receives by triangulating its position on the mobile phone network and performing what's known as a reverse lookup on any wireless networks to which it has access.

Combined, so long as it has coverage, these three location tools let it keep a very accurate fix on its precise position on any part of the globe. Better yet, because each service is complimentary to each of the others, even if only one is accessible at any time it will still be able to turn in a fairly accurate result.

This data is used for a wide range of purposes by a whole host of third-party applications so that they can offer you vouchers and discounts on the basis of your location, walk you step by step through a series of directions, or tag your posts to social networks with your location at the time of writing.

From a photographer's point of view, though, the most relevant use for this data is to tag your images.

By enabling Location Services and giving it access to the camera application it can pinpoint your photos on a map so you always know where they were taken.

that has requested access to your location over time listed below.

You'll notice that in the grab to the left there's a small grey arrow beside Camera. That indicates that the Camera app has used our location in the last 24 hours. If the arrow was purple it would mean that the application was using our location right now, and if it was a hollow purple arrow it would be using what's known as a geofence to monitor our position within a specified area.

Camera doesn't use geofences but they are used by other applications such as Reminders to check when you enter or leave an area.

Once you have enabled Location Services, given the camera access and taken some photos you can start to explore them on the map. Open the Photos application and tap *Places* on the bottom toolbar. You'll see that all the spots where you've taken photos are marked using a red pushpin.

Unpinch on the screen to separate them, then tap on a pin to reveal how many photos were taken there. Tapping the bubble that pops up reveals thumbnails of just those images (*below*).

Tagging them with accurate longitude and latitude geocodes means they can be plotted on a map, both inside the phone itself and when offloaded to external software such as Adobe Lightroom and Apple iPhoto, or to a photo sharing site like Flickr.

This feature isn't turned on by default, so to enable Location Services tap *Settings | Privacy | Location Services* and check that the slider at the top of the screen is set to on (*see above*).

This slider lets you quickly enable or disable all of your location services, with individual controls for each application

iPhone camera alternatives

The iPhone's built-in camera app is fine for general photography, but other than the option to shoot HDR images, display gridlines and shoot panoramas on the iPhone 4S and 5 running iOS 6, it's not greatly versatile.

That's given third-party developers the opportunity to jump in and provide camera alternatives with some surprising, useful extra features.

You can't remove it from the iPhone altogether as it's a core iOS application, or swap out the Camera shortcut that appears on the lock screen, as swiping this up still opens the default camera.

Camera+

Camera+ is much more than just a regular camera. It's an end-to-end iPhone photography suite.

Where snapping your pictures is concerned, though, the most useful features are found by tapping the cog icon beside the shutter release button to open up the four different shooting modes [1]. Three of these – stabilizer, timer and burst – aren't available in the regular iOS camera application.

Stabilizer naturally evens out shaky framing while timing takes multiple

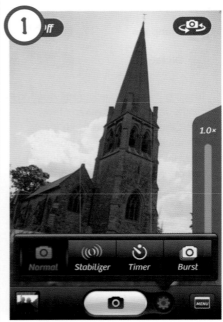

shots in quick succession, although at a lower resolution than the iPhone's native setting. This is useful for capturing fast moving sports shots, kids playing, wildlife and so on.

For taking your own portrait, though, the most useful of them all is almost certainly the timer. Tapping this delays the shutter release by five, 15 or 30 seconds (you choose which by tapping the screen). This lets you prop the camera on a steady surface, fire the shutter and then stroll into the

shot without having to use the lower-resolution front-mounted sensor.

You can save your images either to the regular Camera Roll or to the Camera+ Lightbox [2], and from there share them or use the application's built-in editing features. These are applied on a frame-wide basis so are one-tap operations, and for many of them the process is simplified by picking from a series of thumbnail previews [3].

Camera+ costs 69p and can be downloaded from *http://bit.ly/T2wAKv*

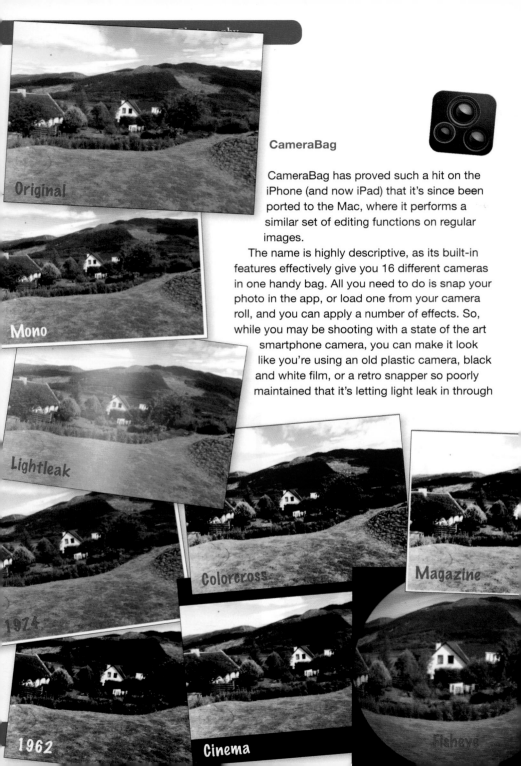

CameraBag

CameraBag has proved such a hit on the iPhone (and now iPad) that it's since been ported to the Mac, where it performs a similar set of editing functions on regular images.

The name is highly descriptive, as its built-in features effectively give you 16 different cameras in one handy bag. All you need to do is snap your photo in the app, or load one from your camera roll, and you can apply a number of effects. So, while you may be shooting with a state of the art smartphone camera, you can make it look like you're using an old plastic camera, black and white film, or a retro snapper so poorly maintained that it's letting light leak in through

Original

Mono

Lightleak

1974

Colorcross

Magazine

1962

Cinema

Fisheye

the edges, thus staining the film with wonderful colour streaks.

You might wonder why you would want to seemingly ruin your photos this way, but in actual fact the result is quite charming, and it affords them a level of analogue authenticity that's missing from many modern digital photos.

Double-tapping a photo once it has had an effect applied makes random changes to the processing, while tapping the small 'i' in the upper corner opens the full options from which you can deactivate specific effects you never want to use, and turn on and off the built-in borders. CameraBag costs £1.49 from *http://bit.ly/Pesown*

Plastic

Lolo

Infrared

Italiano

Instant

Silver

Camera Awesome

Awesome by name, awesome by nature. Camera Awesome seems to plug all the gaps in the native camera application.

For starters, it offers the same burst shooting and timer options as Camera+, so you can capture fast moving subjects and self portraits using the high resolution rear sensor rather than the lower-resolution camera built in to the front of the iPhone case. It also has a shake reduction option and can make the whole screen one enormous shutter button.

However, it goes further than this. The timed shutter option is supplemented by an option to fire off exposures every few seconds so you can easily create a series of time lapse stills that show how things change over time. It's up to you how often it shoots a new picture, but it's easy enough to set by tapping the screen.

There's also a wealth of features for keeping important elements aligned in your image. It uses the iPhone's built-in accelerometer to show you when you are holding your phone level so you know when your horizons are straight, and there are four separate composition options, with the grid of thirds that we already know from the regular camera app supplemented by a golden section, tri-sec and square option so you can get just the result you're after.

Perhaps the smartest tools of all sit firmly on the exposure side of the equation, though, as you can set focus and exposure separately.

When using the regular iOS camera application, a single tap sets the point of focus in your image, and the iPhone simultaneously uses the available light in that position within the frame as its reference point for working out the appropriate exposure setting. Sometimes this isn't appropriate, as it could mean that your subject falls in shadow, or your background is over-exposed and washed out.

Above: Camera Awesome's extensive features include a self timer (left), time lapse option (centre) and a guide that shows you when you are holding the iPhone level.

Right: Once you have taken your picture you can perform a series of edits to improve the result using the built in tools and effects.

Here, on the other hand, you can tap twice to set them independently of each other. First, tap on the main subject of your photo to set the focus. This point will always be sharp, regardless of where you meter for exposure. Now, without taking your finger off the screen, use your thumb or another finger to tap on the point where you would like to measure the correct exposure courtesy of a second on-screen marker.

Camera Awesome is a great iPhone photography tool, and best of all the basic version is free from *http://bit.ly/ VioVzk*

Chapter 3
Editing your photos

Editing with iPhone

iPhoto has long been one of the best photo management apps on the Mac, and now it's available on iOS, too. It's not installed by default, but rather is a paid-for download from the App Store. It's a universal application, so buying on either the iPhone or iPad makes it available on both devices for no additional charge.

On iOS it's naturally been somewhat slimmed down – especially where the iPhone is concerned – but you can still use it to organise your photos into collections, edit them and upload them

to the net to share with friends and family without first having to transfer them back to your Mac or PC.

Here we'll walk you through the most common editing and publishing tasks so that wherever you happen to be you won't have to wait until you get back home to start being creative with your photos.

iPhoto interface

iPhoto files your photos on a series of virtual shelves (see left). You'll notice that the albums on the shelves match the albums in your iPhone's Photos application. To keep them in sync, iPhoto will frequently update your library, which will require that you pause what you're doing for a short time.

The toolbar at the bottom of the screen is where you navigate the different parts of the application, with Albums and Photos being fairly self-explanatory options. The Events entry will only make sense to anyone who uses iPhoto on their Mac, and it mirrors the Events into which photos

iPhoto organises your various albums on a series of glass shelves. New albums are added as you create them, with dedicated smart album containing all of your edited shots.

Events are added to your iPhoto iOS app when you use iTunes to synchronise images from an existing iPhoto library on the Mac. Select the Events you want to copy across by clicking on the Photos tab in the iTunes sync pages.

are organised there. You can decide which of your Mac-based Events are shared with your iPhone when syncing it through iTunes by connecting your iPhone to your Mac or PC with iTunes running and clicking it in the sidebar. When the configuration screen opens, click Photos on the content bar that runs just below the main iTunes status window and select the Events you want to copy across. See the grab above for more information.

The penultimate option inside iPhoto is Journals, which are an iPhoto-exclusive feature through which you can gather together your best photos and publish them online in a digital photo album. These differ considerably from the old Galleries that were available on MobileMe until Apple swapped out the service for iCloud.

The cog at the end of the toolbar opens iPhoto's various options. It's worth taking a look at this, and if you're running out of battery power consider switching off the Wireless Beaming feature as this relies on Bluetooth, which will consume power. This is also where you'll find a link to iPhoto's comprehensive help screens, so if you don't have this guide with you when you're out shooting with your iPhone, turn there first.

Working with photos

To start working with your photos, either tap Photos on the toolbar and select a shot, or open an album from the Albums screen and pick one from there. The latter option is often a quicker way to get to precisely the shot you're after –

particularly if you've organised them into subject groups.

The layout of the screen that follows is determined by the orientation of your phone, with a portrait phone showing a strip of thumbnails for the shots in your album along the bottom of the screen, and a landscape phone showing them in a sidebar column, as you'll see in the screen grab below.

Tap the photo you want to work with and it will be displayed in the larger

Guide: iPhoto image management controls

[1] Tap to open menu and select a range of photos; *[2]* Show / hide thumbnails sidebar or footer; *[3]* Share, print, email or publish the current photo; *[4]* View or edit photo info; *[5]* Swap between original and edited image; *[6]* Open full editing tools.

part of the window, with a range of management tools stripped above it. See below for a run-down of each of those tools and what they do.

The most useful among them at this point are button 4, which lets you view information about how the image was shot and add your own notes (see grab, right), and button 3, which lets you share it using the regular iPhone controls, including emailing, posting it to Twitter and sending it to your Facebook account. We'll explore these in more depath later on. This is also the part of the application to which you'd turn if you wanted to beam the photo over Bluetooth to another iOS device running iPhoto.

Button 5 – the curled up photo – flips backwards and forwards between your original shot and an edited version of the same picture. When you first open an image it doesn't do anything as you won't have made any changes to it so there is no comparison to be made. That's what we'll cover off next, though, so select the image you want to work with, and then tap Edit to start making changes.

As you work with iPhoto you'll notice that it frequently needs to pause and update the library to make sure that all of your recently-added images are ready to edit.

Above: tapping the information button calls up the underlying image metadata with full details of when the photo was shot, what camera you used, its resolution and the camera settings, including aperture and focal length.

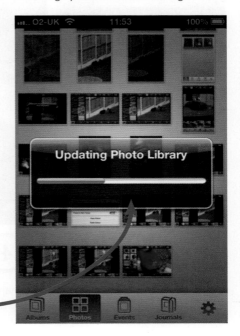

Guide: iPhoto image editing controls

iPhoto's image editing tools are organised within a series of multi-layered menus. The first menu that you see only lets you apply an automatic enhancement control, rotate your image and mark it as a favourite. You can also hide it from here.

To take full advantage of all that iPhoto has to offer in the way of image editing, you need to press the toolbox icon on the left hand end of the toolbar. This reveals the full set of controls, which let you manage brightness, colour and exposure.

[1] Open full editing controls; [2] Auto enhance; [3] Rotate image by 90 degrees (tap to turn it further); [4] Flag for follow up; [5] Set as a favourite; [6] Hide this photo; [7] Open settings and options; [8] The toolbox icon indicates that image has been edited.

Guide: Image editing menus

[1] Crop and rotate, allows you to change the composition of your shot by dragging in the borders and use a wheel to change the orientation to correct uneven horizon lines.

[2] Open exposure menu to change the brightness of the image and play with the highlights and shadows.

[3] Open colour menu so that you can adjust specific tones or change the overall saturation of the image, either by dragging on colour blocks at the bottom of the screen or interacting with the image directly.

[4] Open adjustment brushes so that you can apply changes in a piecemeal fashion by literally painting on the area to which the adjustment should apply.

[5] Open effects options and choose from a range of preset image effects, varying the strength of each one by picking from a stepped scale.

Technique: Cropping and rotating images in iPhoto

Drag the handles on each corner of the image to crop in on the main subject area of your photo. The guide lines divide your photos into thirds and help you to maintain a balanced composition. Pinching and unpinching zooms the photo.

Tap here to constrain the image's proportions

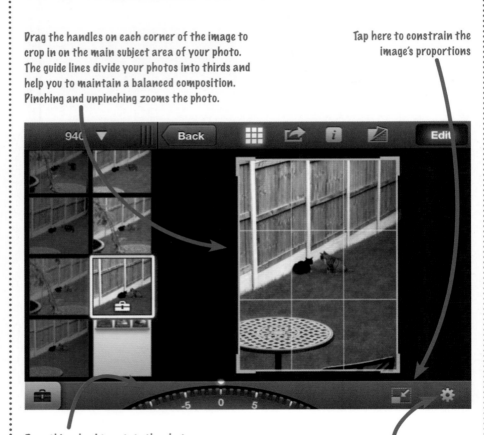

Drag this wheel to rotate the photo and correct uneven horizons. Your image will automatically resize itself to fill the crop selection area so that you don't end up with blank spaces inside the frame. Parts extending beyond it are cropped.

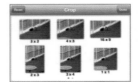

The cog lets you quickly select a range of pre-set crop sizes with previews of each result (see grab, left)

Editing photos

When you enter the editing mode, turn your attention to the new toolbar that appears at the bottom of the screen. This gives you access to all of iPhoto's creative controls.

The main toolbar, explained on page 48, contains only one real editing tool, which lets you apply an automated enhancement to the active photo (see grab, right), as determined by iPhoto itself. Often this will be enough to improve your image as far as it needs to be, but if you want to take things further then simply tap button 1 – the toolbox – to open the full editing tools.

The tools have been designed to be extremely easy to use. They require no real knowledge of image manupulation and are all managed through simple taps, pinches and twists, just like most other iOS applications.

The first toolbar, shown on page 52, lets you crop your images by dragging their edges in towards the centre, or open up secondary toolbars using other buttons.

Exposure presents you with a simple toolbar through which you can change the balance between light and dark, or tweak the contrast and brightness. You can make similar changes directly by tapping on the photo. Adjust the highlights, for example, by tapping and dragging left and right or up and down

Auto-Enhance tasks iPhoto with applying the most appropriate adjustments to your image to realise its full potential.

on the brightest part of the image, and do the same with the darkest part to work on the shadows.

The Colour control lets you change the tone of your image, again by dragging sliders or parts of the image directly (see the four-way arrow in the grab on the next page).

Each of these changes takes effect across the whole image, so you should be careful with precisely how your edits are being applied. Specifically you should try and make sure that the people in your images don't have unrealistic skin tones as this will be immediately obvious. The easiest way to do this is to instruct iPhoto to preserve skin tones by opening the tool options by clicking the cog icon and tapping the slider beside Preserve Skin Tones so that it is set to ON.

Technique: colour-correcting your photos

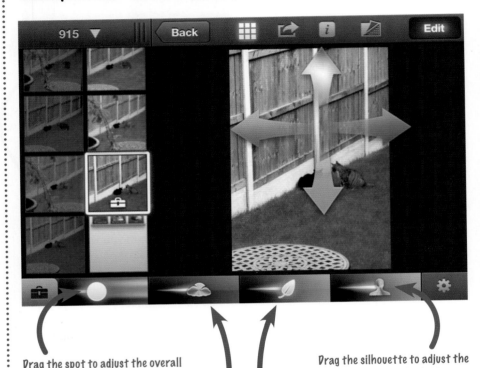

Drag the spot to adjust the overall saturation of your image. The further you drag to the right, the punchier your colours become, but be careful not to take it too far.

Drag the cloud to adjust the blueness of skies in your image, but bear in mind that other blue elements in your image may also be affected, such as water, paintwork and clothing.

Drag the silhouette to adjust the warmth of your image. Cooler images have a blue tint while warmer colours are more yellow or red. Dragging to the right makes them warmer.

Drag the leaf to adjust the greenery in your image, such as grass, trees and plants. Bear in mind that any of these adjusted colours may appear within others, such as moss on bark.

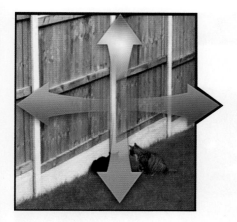

You don't have to drag on the sliders to adjust the individual tones in your image. You can also put your finger directly on the photo and drag to change the colours that appear below it. The four-way arrow shows you what you will change. In the grab above, dragging vetically increases and decreases the saturation while dragging left and right adjusts the greens.

Copying and pasting colours

When you have applied whatever changes you need to correct the colours in an image, you can paste the same adjustments to other images shot at the same time. Pick Copy Colour (see right), switch to your other image, and then tap the cog followed by Paste Colour.

White balance and skin tones

The white balance setting lets you specify what the lighting conditions were like when you shot your image. This will affect the overall look of your finished picture as iPhoto will compensate by adjusting the tones in the photo in such a way that it would know that a piece of white card shot under that lighting really would look white. In theory this should make all of the tones in your image more accurately replicate their real-life colours at the point when you shot them. You can access the white balance setting by tapping the cog on the far right of the colour correction toolbar.

You will also find the option to preserve skin tones on this screen. Switching this on allows you to make changes on a frame-wide basis, safe in the knowledge that it shouldn't detrimentally affect peoples' faces and other exposed areas of skin..

Technique: correcting exposure and contrast

The exposure and contrast control consists of a single but very versatile slider through which you can make a series of very useful, measured adjustments to your image. Unless you use one of the adjustment brushes, all of your changes are applied to the whole of your image at once, so be sure to watch the photo as you drag the slider between the shadow and highlight markers at either end of the scale.

Dragging the central slider to the right increases the overall brightness in the image (see [1] below). Notice that whenever you make a change to the central slider the two to either side of it adjust at the same time so that the one on the left always sits half way between the slider you're adjusting and complete black, while the one sits half way between your current position and complete white.

Dragging the central slider to the left, therefore, darkens the image by giving more prominence to the shadows within the shot [2].

You can also drag the central markers that sit between the sun icon and the highlight and shadow extremes. Notice how in images [3] and [4] dragging just one slider on either side has caused its partner on the opposite side to move the same distance in the opposite direction. This has allowed us to very quickly

increase the contrast in image [3] while decreasing the level of contrast in image [4].

You can also drag the very extremes of the scale so that the highlight or shadow markers move in towards the centre of the scale. Depending on which you drag you will either make all of your darker tones black or your lighter tones white. Because this could reduce the amount of information retained within your image, iPhoto warns by colouring the end of the scale red (see above).

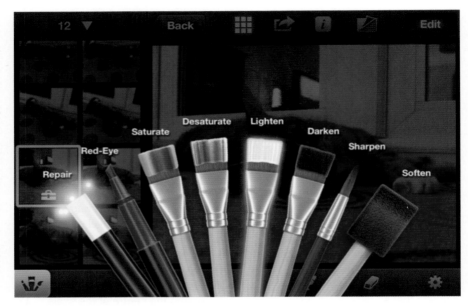

Selective editing

So far we have applied our changes on a frame-wide basis to the whole of each image. However, you can also apply some images selectively to only specific parts of the image by using the adjustment brushes. Again, these are called up from the toolbar.

There are eight brushes in the toolbox, each of which performs a different function (see grab, above). With careful use of the Lighten or Darken brushes you can apply exposure changes to specific parts of your image; likewise, you can apply more controlled adjustments to

the colours in your image using the Saturate and Desaturate brushes.

To work with these brushes, select one and then paint on the parts of your image to which you want to apply the result, leaving the other parts clear.

It's difficult to see which parts of the image you have painted over when using any of these brushes in their default state, but iPhoto includes an option to highlight the parts of the image you have selected. To activate this, tap the cog icon to open each brush's settings pane and make sure that the sider beside Show Strokes is

set to ON. The brush will then lay down red strokes to show you where it has been applied so that you can make sure you have covered every part of the image that you need to edit (the grab, above, shows this in action).

This highlighting is helpful in allowing you to see when you have painted on some parts of the image that you need to leave untouched. If you have done this, tap the eraser and use it to clear parts you want to leave untouched. If you have made a serious error and you need to remove more than half of the strokes it may be easier

to start again; tap the cog and select the option to Erase All.

This menu is also the place where you should turn to specify the strength of your adjustment (see below).

Technique: iPhoto effects

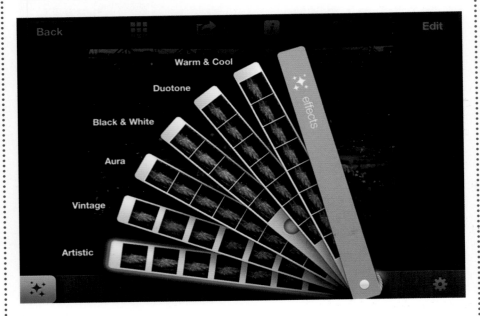

iPhoto's built-in effects let you quickly make common changes to your images without having to step through each of the adjustment screens or use the brushes. There are six effects to choose from covering most of the amendments you might want to make to a shot.

To use them you simply select the one you want to use and the fan will collapse to the toolbar (see below) with your selected effect in place.

The bar that sits on top of it shows how extreme a change you have made, with different parts of the scale having a different effect on the picture.

Some of the effects, such as the black and white effect on the toolbar below, also have supplementary controls to the right. In this case, the first dot applies a vignette effect to draw the eye to the centre. The third is a sepia tone wash.

Sharing your work

When you have finished editing your photos, tapping Edit takes you back to the image management screens, and from here you can share them with your friends and family.

The easiest way to do this is obviously to email, Tweet or post them to Facebook using the regular iOS controls. However, iPhoto also allows you to create more impressive Journals, each of which can contain up to 200 images.

To create a Journal, start by tapping the share shortcut on the management toolbar, followed by Journal. Tap Choose... and then select each of

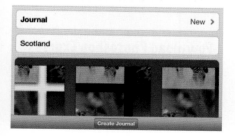

the images you want to include in the Journal by tapping on them one at a time. Each one will be ticked to show that it's been selected (see above).

When you have identified all of the images you want to use, tap Next and give your new Journal a name, then scroll through the six different album designs until you find one that you like.

This is the last step, so tap Create Journal, followed by Show to preview it. If it looks the way you intended you can use it as a slideshow, sent it to iTunes or share it online. If you want to share it online, tap the Share shortcut button again and select iCloud as the destination, followed by the ON/OFF slider.

Editing in Adobe Photoshop Express

Photoshop Express is a free download. That probably sounds too good to be true when you consider how much the full-blown Photoshop image editing application costs and Windows on a Mac... but that's only half true.

While Adobe is clearly using the free download as a way to drive sales of add-on effects and tools, the complimentary application itself is surprisingly powerful and extremely easy-to-use.

Photoshop Express started life as a Flash-based application on the Internet, which was used by many blog editors

to tweak their images prior to uploading them to their sites. When Adobe decided to port it to the iPhone and iPad, though, it had to rewrite it from the ground up, as the iPhone is famed for not running Flash. The result is a sprightly, responsive and highly capable application that's perfect for making quick and surprisingly sophisticated edits on the go, without the cost of upgrading to iPhoto.

Adobe Photoshop Express can work either with images you take directly inside the application or previously-shot photos stored on your Camera Roll or synchronised through Photo Stream. Your first task on launching it is therefore to decide where the asset you're going to edit should be drawn from. We've selected an image from our Camera Roll that we'd taken previously and now want to edit before uploading it to the web (see left).

Editing in Adobe Photoshop Express

The first thing you'll notice when you take or open a photo are the two

> ### Download Photoshop Express
>
> Photoshop Express is a free download from the App Store. Simply point your browser at http://bit.ly/QUaJZj

Tap to open the sharing menu, which lets you send your image to common social networks or email (see right)

Tap here to open your image in the Photoshop Express editing environment to make changes before sharing

buttons at the bottom of the screen. The first, the box with the arrow pointing out of it, is the Share control. This lets you upload your image directly to Facebook, Twitter, Flickr, or Tumblr, send it to photoshop.com for further work or email it to your contacts.

If you want to edit your image before sharing it, tap the pencil icon to open the editing tools.

Photoshop Express editing tools

The editing tools are broken down into four primary categories. The buttons for each of these run across the top of the screen. They are, in turn, cropping and orientation (the double set square icon), luminance, which incorporates

exposure, tint, saturation and so on (the sun icon), filters (the half shaded circle), and effects and borders (the stars).

Tapping any one of these drops down a menu from which you can select sub options. Notice that in the menu the over the page, where we have dropped

Below: The four buttons on the toolbar give you access to every editing feature bundled as part of Photoshop Express.

Beware that some of the features on the menus are premium entries and require a further purchase. They're indicated by a plus and corner chip.

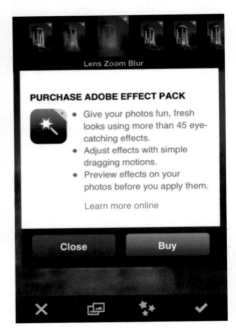

down the filters menu, the last option – Reduce Noise – has a plus in one corner (above). This indicates that the tool is a premium element that must be bought separately as an upgrade.

You can still use it, but before you save the results you need to make an in-app purchase. We'll come to this when we look at effects and borders, later.

At the bottom of the screen there are four other buttons, (see [1] opposite page). The cross cancels the current editing operation, the backwards- and forwards-pointing arrows undo and redo your last operation, and the

down pointing arrow touching a block saves your edited photo.

Any time you're working on an image, you'll see three other icons in this space (see [2] opposite page). Again, the cross, which sits on the far left, cancels the edit. Holding down on the two overlaid frames at the centre of the toolbar calls up the original image again so that you can compare what

Many controls have been split so that dragging horizontally applies one effect, while dragging vertically applies another, as seen here.

you started with to what you have now, and the tick on the far right of the bar applies your edit.

All of the tools work on a frame-wide basis and are controlled simply by dragging up and down or left and right on the screen.

For example, in the image to the right we have selected the brightness and contrast tool from the second drop-down menu – luminance. The individual controls for brightness and contrast have been split out so that dragging to the left darkens the image and dragging to the right lightens it. At the same time, dragging down reduces the contrast in the image, and dragging up increases it. Because we don't need to put our fingers on the actual bars themselves at the top and left edges of the screen, we can simultaneously make the image both brighter and with a sharper contrast by putting a finger somewhere around the centre and dragging up and diagonally to the right.

Likewise, we could increase the brightness and reduce the contrast by dragging down diagonally to the right, and so on.

Some effects, such as this one, are applied in real time, so dragging slowly will allow you to see the effect you're having live, as you make your changes. If you drag too quickly, you'll find that Photoshop Express has to pause for a moment while it updates the picture to take account of the more extreme adjustment.

Some adjustments, however, don't require that you work in two directions.

Some tools, such as Straighten (left), don't require that you apply changes to any more than one aspect, and even those that do, such as Hue and Saturation (right) can be applied so that only one half has any bearing on the finished image.

The straighten tool, for example, which is found in the first drop-down menu, requires only that you rotate the image on screen and then tap the tick (see grab, above).

Even those tools that do call up two adjustments simultaneously, such as Hue and Saturation, or Brightness and Contrast, can be used so that adjustments are made to only one element at a time. For example, in the image to the right, above, we have adjusted the hue of the frame so that the green grass is now purple and the blue sky is yellow, but we have not played at all with the saturation, so the tones, while unnatural, are not unduly prominent within the picture and the overall balance is maintained.

Effects and borders

Open the fourth menu – effects and borders – and you'll find a healthy selection of graphical treatments ready to be dropped onto your image. However, beware that this is one area in which you are most likely to find yourself applying adjustments for which you might be asked to pay. Fortunately, you're not committed to buying them just because you've applied them to

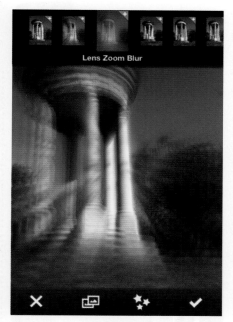

This Lens Zoom Blur effect looks great, but it's a premium filter that you'll have to pay for if you want to save it.

corner and the plus symbol, which as we learned from the drop-down menus indicates that this is a premium effect.

Tapping the tick button to apply it to our image brings up a request to buy the Adobe Effect Pack, which unlocks this blur effect and 44 others. If we don't want to buy it, we simply tap close to return to our image, but if we tap the tick again to exit, we just get back to this screen. The only option if we don't want to buy it is to tap the cross and cancel the edit altogether.

If you don't want to spend any money, then, confine yourself to using only those borders and effects that appear on the top row of options in either module.

Saving your work

Once you have finished making your edits, you need to save your work back to your camera roll. To do this, simply tap the down-pointing arrow and it will be sent back to your Camera Roll.

Although it doesn't say so when saving, Photoshop Express actually saves a completely new version of the image in the Camera Roll rather than overwriting the original, so if you want to start again and make a whole different set of changes, simply return to the beginning, open a second copy of the original image and let your imagination run wild.

your image; you only have to spend if you want to save the result.

The free effects and borders that come bundled as part of Adobe Photoshop Express are all on the top line of the various menus. Tap one to apply it to your image and drag up and down on the screen to adjust the strength of the finished result.

In the image above, we have applied the Lens Zoom Blur effect and dragged down the screen to reduce it slightly so that we still have a fairly clear image in the background. Notice, though, that the preview thumbnail at the top of the screen is overlaid by a colour chip

Editing photos with Snapseed

Snapseed may not be as well known as either Photoshop or iPhoto, but that doesn't mean it's lacking in features.

This sophisticated iPhone image editing tool lets you go beyond frame-wide editing options to tweak specific parts of an image, allowing you to apply localised adjustments to change the balance and focus of specific portions of an image.

Snapseed includes a wide variety of adjustment types, and each is grouped with similar types. So, you'll find brighness, ambience, contrast and saturation grouped together since they're each common editing controls rather than applied effects.

Dragging up and down on the screen always lets you change the selected adjustment from a menu that pops up on the fly, while dragging left and right respectively decreases and increases the strength of the adjustment or effect.

Naturally you can also pinch and unpinch to change the level of zoom.

Some effects can be applied to just a specific area within your image. The selected area is chosen by dropping a control point, which works in a similar manner to the control points employed by Adobe Lightroom and Apple Aperture. You can change the size of the area affected in much the same way that you change the strength of the effect, which makes Snapseed one of the most flexible editing tools going.

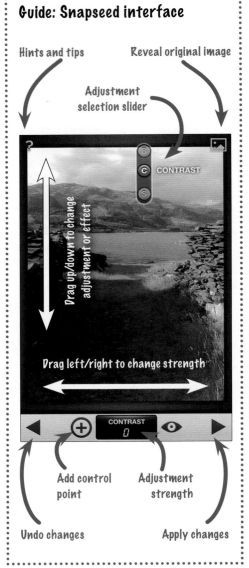

Guide: Snapseed interface

Hints and tips

Reveal original image

Adjustment selection slider

Drag up/down to change adjustment or effect

CONTRAST

Drag left/right to change strength

CONTRAST
0

Add control point

Adjustment strength

Undo changes

Apply changes

Workthrough: Editing photos in Snapseed

[1] Open your image by tapping the library button, or take a new picture using the camera option to get yourself started. Each of Snapseed's effects and adjustments is organised into a group and filed in one of the packages that runs across the bottom of the display. Here we've opened a fairly ordinary shot of a causeway running down to a loch. We're going to use the effects and adjustments to make it look very old.

[2] First we have selected the Selective Adjustment pack. This lets us drop control points onto the image by tapping the '+' button. Each control point can adjust brightness, contrast or saturation; we select between them by dragging up and down, as illustrated in the guide box to the left. Here we have dropped two control points on the sky and grass, and dragged left on the sky to darken it off, and right on the grass to brighten it.

Workthrough continued: Editing photos in Snapseed (2)

[3] Tapping the right arrow applies our previous adjustment and lets us move on to the next one. Here we have opted for the Image Tune adjustment that gives us control over brightness, ambiance, contrast, saturation and white balance. Dragging up and down on the screen lets us select which effect we want to work with, so we have dragged until the saturation option is brought to the front and highlighted by a blue bar.

[4] We now drag left and right to adjust the strength of the effect. We don't want to remove all of the colour from our image, but we do want to tone things down slightly so that in the finished product there is only a hint of colour and it appears that it has faded badly over time, as old photos were prone to do. Dragging left reduces the saturation within the image. As you move your finger, the readout at the bottom of the interface is copied within the image.

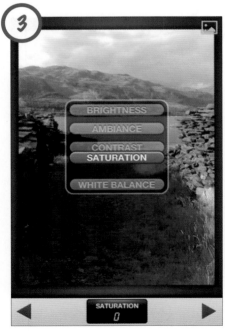

[5] Now we're ageing the edge of our photo. We've dragged along to the end of the run of adjustment options installed in our copy of Snapseed and tapped on Frames. The frame we are using here has very ragged edges and makes it look both like the printing was quite imperfect, and that it has been battered over time. Dragging right in this instance doesn't adjust the strength of the effect, but the width of the frame. Dragging left makes it narrower.

[6] Our image is starting to get where we want to take it, but despite the slightly faded colours and the ragged edge it's still not looking quite old enough. So, we've opened the grunge adjustment to make it dirty. Tapping the crossed arrows randomises the pattern of the dirt in the image, while the grid to the right selects from pre-defined textures. Dragging left and right adjusts the strength of the dirt and how much of the image shows through.

Workthrough continued: Editing photos in Snapseed (3)

[7] The last effect we'll apply comes from the Drama pack, which we'll use to knock up the strength of our adjustments and bring out some detail within the path. Compare this image, with the filter strength set to 79, to the one in step 6, and you'll see that there is much more definition in the ground areas, which previously were lost to the shadows. This is our last effect. Tapping the right arrow takes us back one last time, after which we can use the picture.

[8] The options open to us when it comes to using our picture are very familiar, and accessed by tapping the regular shortcut button (the rectangle with the curved arrow coming out of it). The simplest option is obviously to save the result back to the Photo Library as a new image, but we can also post it to Flickr or Instagram, neither of which are options built into iOS 6, email it or post it to the iPhone's social networks of choice: Facebook and Twitter.

Before and After

Without employing any advanced photo editing skills, Snapseed has enabled us to make some pretty extreme adjustments to our image. We have taken a balanced, well exposed image as shot by the iPhone and corrected using the built-in HDR filter, and applied a number of degrading adjustments to simulate the effect of ageing on a regular printed photo.

Download SnapSeed

SnapSeed is a £2.99 download from the App Store. Simply point your browser at http://itunes.com/apps/snapseed/

Before

After

Editing photos in PhotoGene2

PhotoGene2 bills itself as a collage maker, but it is also a highly accomplished photo editing tool. It's also extremely competitively-priced.

Many of its tools, such as curves control, histogram and professional handling of saturation, dodging and clarity, each of which we'll use in the walkthrough that follows, come close to rivalling what you'd expect to see in a regular desktop image editing application.

The interface is beautifully crafted and easy to use, with rotating wheels switching between the various tools, and almost all adjustments controlled by dragged sliders.

Perhaps best of all, PhotoGene2 skilfully mixes both frame-wide adjustments and more localised retouching options to give you complete control over the finished picture.

Download PhotoGene2

PhotoGene2 is a 69p download from the App Store. Simply point your browser at http://bit.ly/TO7hsj

Guide: PhotoGene2 Interface

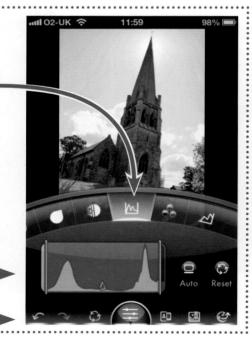

Drag the tool selector to the left and right to cycle through the available editing controls open to you.

The main working area below the tools selector is where you'll make your adjustments. In some cases, as here, there's an Auto option that tasks PhotoGene2 with making the best possible adjustments on your behalf. On other times you'll drag sliders to affect your changes. Notice the Reset button – that undoes any changes you have made with the current tool.

The bottom toolbar switches between editing modes and sharing options.

Walkthrough: Editing photos in PhotoGene2

Over the next four pages we'll walk through the process of correcting this poorly-exposed photo of a church. At the start of the process, the strong sunlight behind the spire has thrown the rest of the building into shadow, but by the end we have rebalanced the image so that both the building itself and the grass in front of it are clearer and better defined, without adversely affecting the overall balance of the composition.

Before

After

Walkthrough: Editing photos in PhotoGene2 continued

[1] Here's our starting point. The composition is quirky, thanks to the skewed horizon, and we could fix that in PhotoGene if we chose, but in this instance it makes for a more interesting frame overall, so we'll leave it as it is. What we really want to do is fix the lighting. At the moment, the church and the grass in front of it are either in silhouette or shadow as the position of the sun behind the spire has brightened the sky. We'll focus our attention on bringing out detail in those areas.

[2] As with many editing applications PhotoGene lets you either open an image that's already in place in your Photo Library or take a new shot using the iPhone's camera and work on it directly. We've opened one from the library. On the bottom toolbar, the first two buttons undo and redo an action, the third reverts to the original, the fifth compares the edit to the original image, sixth opens the underlying data and the last publishes it. The tools are behind the large central button.

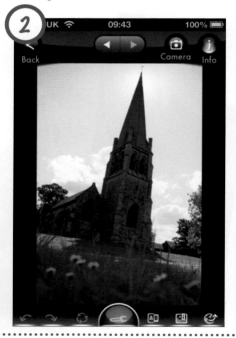

[3] Here we've tapped the sixth button to open the underlying image data. This calls up various information about the photo and lets us apply further data ourselves, such as a rating. Tapping through the buttons at the top of the screen switches between the different data views, many of which will have been set by the camera at the point when the image was captured. Specifically, Exif records shooting conditions and GPS naturally records the image location.

[4] Before we start work on the edit we want to attach some extra data to our image so that when we publish it online or share it with friends it is properly identified as our work. We'll do this by tapping on the IPTC button and then using the fields below to add our new information.

IPTC stands for International Press Telecommunications Council, and is used as a shorthand for the series of standard data fields used to describe images in the media.

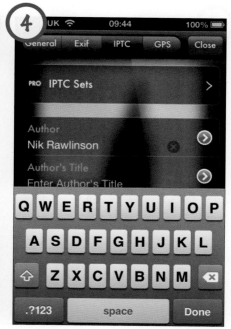

Walkthrough: Editing photos in PhotoGene2 continued

[5] With our data in place it's time to start work on editing the image. Start by tapping the tools button at the centre of the bottom toolbar. This calls up a range of familiar options, with crop allowing us to trim the image so that we can change the composition, rotate spinning it around, and so on. The option we want is Retouches, which gives us access to the complete set of editing tools open to the PhotoGene2 user that allow for more selective editing of specific parts of the frame.

[6, 7 and 8] The range of adjustment tools open to us is impressive, and comes close to matching many desktop and laptop image editing applications. We want to start by brightening our shadows, so will use the dodge tool.

Dodging is a method used in traditional print making to restrict the amount of light falling on the sensitive paper used to develop film-based photographs. The developer would use a piece of card to block out some of the light for a part of the exposure time,

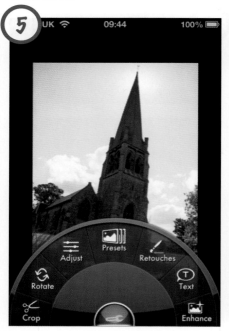

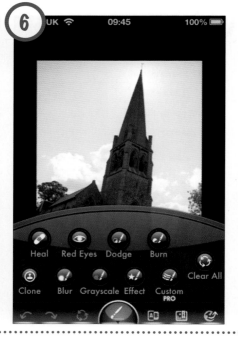

thus effectively exposing the blocked, or 'dodged', part of the image less than the other sections. This meant that the paper didn't turn as dark here as it did elsewhere, and so the result was a lighter print in those parts.

In step [7] we have used the dodge tool's default settings to brighten up the grass and the lower part of the church tower, but as things stand the brush is too broad to accurately dodge the point of the spire without also dodging parts of the neighbouring sky.

We have therefore tapped the Options button at the top of the screen and, in step [8], we're dragging the radius slider to the left to reduce the size of the brush, and the feather slider to the right to harden off the edges so that we can get a nice crisp finish to the spire's roofing tiles.

Having resized our brush we'll now tap on the image again to dismiss the options panel and continue dodging the spire, with the finer control now enabling us to get to the very tip.

Walkthrough: Editing photos in PhotoGene2 continued

[9] We have brought out a lot of the previously missing detail in our image with our dodging exercise, and could now do with brightening the foreground as a whole. However, we don't want to affect the sky, which is already bright enough as it stands. Return to the overall tools view and select Adjust, then Curves. Dragging up the centre of the curve brightens the whole frame, so we'll add a second control point in the top quarter to pin the highlights in place and stop them from being brightened.

[10] Our image is already looking a lot better, but brightening it that way has slightly washed out the colours. We want to reinstate some of its previous punch, so we've dragged the wheel above the tools to the right until we reach the saturation and vibrance sliders, and dragged the saturation control to the right to increase the strength of the colours in the frame. Be careful not to over-egg the pudding here, as over-strong colours can look unrealistic and false.

[11] Finally, we want to give our image greater presence, so we've dragged the tool selection wheel to the furthest right position to reveal the Clarity control. This increases the level of detail in the image, but again must be used with care as applying the effect too strongly will result in an unrealistic image. Overuse of the Clarity control will accentuate your contrasts and can introduce white haloes around dominant elements in your image, such as the spire where it passes in front of the sky.

[12] We've finished editing our image and it's now time to put it to use. PhotoGene gives you a wide range of export options, including sending it to other devices, posting to Facebook, Twitter, Instagram or Flickr, and even transfering it ot a remote computer or server using FTP (File Transfer Protocol). Don't skip straight to the export options at the bottom of the screen, though; also work your way through the watermark, resolution and IPTC options up top to protect your work.

Sharing your photos with Instagram

Instagram is a phone-based social networking service dedicated to sharing photos with followers. Although you can view photos online through the direct links to the Instagram website, you only get the full benefit of its following and subscribing features if you access it through the iPhone or Android client.

It's now owned by Facebook, but the fact it's been snapped up by an enormous social network hasn't done much to change the features that its loyal subscribers appreciate.

It has always had a rather low-fi feel, and that persists in the latest updates. Any image you post to the service is cropped into a square format that is highly reminiscent of the picture shape in the output of an old-fashioned instant camera (hence the name).

You can go further than this, though, and also apply a series of old-school retro filters that make your image look a lot older than it actually is (see the examples on the opposite page).

The idea is that you follow other people, and they follow you, and that in just the same way that updates other people post to Twitter show up on your

Instagram is a phone-based social network for sharing photos. It offers several effects and formats your images like an old-fashioned instant camera.

timeline, so photos posted to Instagram appear automatically in your client. In reverse, your pictures also show up in the client apps of those who are following you.

It's worth downloading even if you don't know anyone else on Instagram, though, as the effects are fun to play with, you can post links to your Instagram feed simultaneously to your Twitter and Facebook accounts.

Download Instagram

Instagram is a free download from the App Store. Simply point your browser at http://itunes.com/apps/instagram/

Instagram's integrated filters

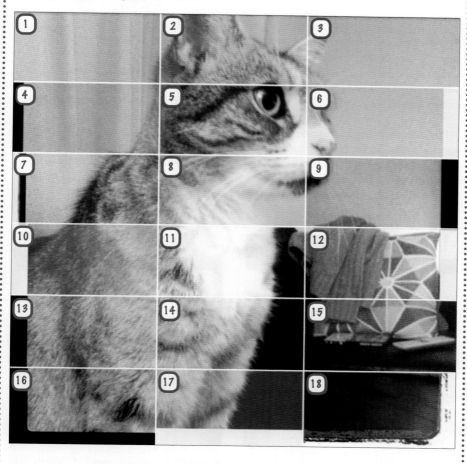

[1] Normal   [2] Amaro   [3] Rise   [4] Hudson   [5] X-Pro II
[6] Sierra   [7] Lo-fi   [8] Earlybird   [9] Sutro   [10] Toaster
[11] Brannan   [12] Inkwell   [13] Walden   [14] Hefe   [15] Valencia
[16] Nashville   [17] 1977   [18] Kelvin

Technique: Posting photos to Instagram

Part of Instagram's popularity is the fact that it's very easy to use. Posting an image is therefore a simple process of walking through just four steps, as we'll outline here.

[1] By default, Instagram expects you to take a new photo, but you can also use one that's already in your library, as we are doing here, by tapping the double overlaid squares at the bottom of the opening screen. Once you have selected the image you want to post, pinch and unpinch until the section you want to use fits neatly in the square at the centre of the screen, and then tap the Choose button.

[2] You can now apply some pre-set adjustments to give it a bit of style. Scroll through the style options at the bottom of the screen until you find one

you like, tap on it and then tap the tick to apply it to the image.

[3] Apply your final adjustments. The sun icon on the bottom toolbar balances the tones in the image and the frame icon top left applies or removes a frame to your image. Here we are adjusting the level of focus in the image. We've tapped the droplet icon on the top bar and selected horizontal focus control,

and are in the process of dragging the focal zone up and down the image to direct our viewer's attention.

[4] When you've finished editing your image, it's time to post it. Tap the tick, then add a short caption, decide whether or not you want it to be located on your Instagram map, and optionally set it to share simultaneously to Twitter, Facebook, Tumblr and other networks.

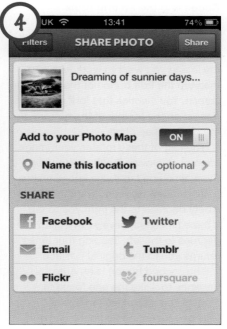

Editing directly in the Photos app

Although you'll get far more choice and flexibility when it comes to making edits if you buy a dedicated image editing app like iPhoto, you shouldn't overlook the basic tools built-in to the Photos application that comes as part of iOS.

You can't selectively change the brightness of individual parts of an image or apply retro filters the way you can with some other apps, but you can crop your images before emailing them to friends, correct redeye problems and apply a general enhancement across the whole frame.

Accessing the editing tools

The tools can be used on any image in your library. Open the Photos app, tap the image you want to work with and then tap the Edit button at the top of the screen. You'll notice that four new icons appear on the toolbar at the bottom of the display (see right).

The first of these rotates your image counter clockwise by ninety degrees. Every time you tap it, the image makes a quarter turn, so if you want to turn it ninety degrees to the right you to tap it three times, effectively turning it 270 degrees to the left. Tapping four times returns you to the original position.

The second button is an Auto Enhance tool like the one found in iPhoto. This examines the overall tone of your image and balances out

Rotate image one turn counter-clockwise by 90 degrees with every tap.

Apply an automatic enhancement to the whole image. There's no user-defined level of control or strength setting here.

Crop the image in a freeform manner or in line with common ratios.

Remove red-eye from the image. This requires a little intervention from yourself to identify the problem eyes.

the various colours and levels of light to produce a more impactful and impressive result. You can't change the degree to which it does this or force it to focus on particular elements of the image such as just the colours or just the illumination, so you rather have to take it at face value. If you don't like the result it produces, tap it again to turn off Auto Enhance.

The third button eliminates redeye in your image – but requires a degree of manual intervention. The Photos app can't tell for itself where the eyes appear in your image. Just looking for a scarlet tone indicative of reflected blood wouldn't work either, as there's no guarantee that what it picks out might not be a piece of decoration or jewellery of the same colour.

Once you have tapped the redeye tool you therefore need to tap on each red eye in the image to show it where

it should apply the correction. If it finds the requisite colour in that position it will neutralise it to remove it from your subject's eyes. If not, it will tell you that it has been unable to find a red eye to heal and ask you can try again.

The final tool, which looks like two set squares pushed against one another, is the crop tool. Tap this and your image will be shrunk slightly on the screen and overlaid by a 3×3 grid. The corners of the grid have thicker borders, and dragging these or the sides towards the centre of the frame or the opposite edge or corner lets you select which part of the image you want to keep. When you let go, the image will be enlarged so that only the selected portion appears on the screen. You can still drag them back out again if you've taken things too far.

You'll notice that there's a constrain button at the bottom of the screen. This lets you restrict the aspect ratio in

Every tap of the rotate button spins your image counter-clockwise by 90 degrees.

Above: Although you have to give the Photos app a helping hand when tasking it with removing red eye problems in your images, it is clever enough to know if you've tapped in the wrong place.

Left: The Auto-Enhance tool, which also appears in iPhoto, examines the colours and lighting in an image and applies a set of adjustments that should make it more balanced and appealing.

which the crop is permitted to act. So, if you want to retain the image's original proportions, drag the crop box until you have selected roughly the area you're after, then tap Constrain and Original.

Other constrain options let you crop to a square, traditional 3×2 and 3×4 ratios, 8×10, 3×5 and 5×7, which mimic paper prints, and an elongated 16×9 aspect ratio, which is the ratio used by many widescreen TVs.

Once you have defined the area you want to keep in this way, tap the yellow Crop button to trim your image.

Having performed the edits you want to make to the picture, use the Save button at the top of the screen to write them to your image library. Be careful, though, as doing so overwrites the original image rather than saving a second copy with your amendments.

The Photos application doesn't make allowances for making a copy of your original before performing these edits, so only conduct them on your originals if you're absolutely certain you are happy to make irrevocable changes.

Get-out clause

If you do discover you have edited one of your original images and you want to

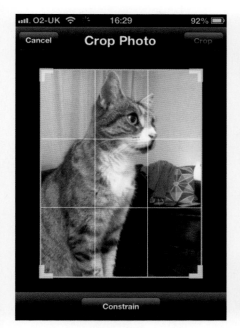
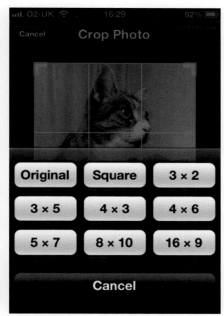

The crop tool simply requires that you drag in the corners or edges of your image towards the centre to specify the area that you want to keep. Tapping the Constrain button opens up a menu of common photo size ratios.

retrieve the unedited version, you may be in luck if you have Photo Stream running on your iPhone. This should have copied the original photo up to iCloud from where you can retrieve it.

To do this, either start iPhoto or Aperture on your Mac and update the iCloud synchronisation, or open the downloads folder on your Windows PC to which iCloud content is copied and drag out the original. Alternatively, open iCloud on your iPhone.

You'll find your iCloud Photo Stream by tapping back to the Albums overview in the Photos app and tapping Photo Stream on the toolbar at the bottom of the screen. From here, tap My Photo Stream and scroll back through the contents until you find the original unedited version of your image. It will only be present in the stream if it was one of the last 1000 images you took – including screen grabs – and was shot within the last 30 days.

Photo Stream

Photo Stream is an integral part of iCloud, which is accessible to anyone using an iPhone, iPad or iPod touch running iOS 5 or later. The idea is quite simple, which is why it's so brilliant.

Previously, every time you took a picture with your iPhone, you had to think about how you were going to get it off your device. Usually it was easiest to simply email it back to yourself, but this was clumsy and could eat into your monthly data allowance if you did it over your 3G connection.

Alternatively you could set up iTunes so that it synchronised your photos every time you connected your device to your computer, but that would mean not only that you'd have to sync more frequently, but also that you'd run

the risk of losing your photos if you misplaced your iPhone in the interim.

Photo Stream solves all of these problems by sending each of your photos to Apple's iCloud servers as soon as you take them. The servers store your most recently-shot 1000 images, taken over the last 30 days. When you exceed 1000 images, the older ones are removed to make way for new additions, and any that are older than 30 days are removed in turn.

There is no web interface, so you can't view your raw Photo Stream online (we'll show you later how you can share a Photo Stream on the web) because Photo Stream isn't designed primarily as a publishing service. It is, instead, a synchronisation tool that copies your photos between each device.

Tip: Signing up for iCloud

Photo Stream requires an iCloud account through which it can sync your photos. iCloud accounts are free, and you probably signed up for one at the point where you first turned on your iPhone or upgraded iOS. They use the same login credentials as the iTunes and iOS Stores. To make sure iCloud is active on your iPhone tap Settings | iCloud and check the Account line (see right).

Apple's Photo Stream service synchronises your 1000 most recently-shot images that are less than 30 days old, between each of your iOS devices and a Mac or PC.

Once your images are on the server, each of your other iOS, OS X and Windows devices that are logged in to the same iCloud account check in with the service periodically to see whether any new images have appeared. Any that they spot will be immediately downloaded and stored in that device's own Photo Stream album within its Photos application. On the Mac, Photo Stream is synchronised with iPhoto or Aperture; on Windows it is synchronised using a set of folders on your hard disk.

Enabling Photo Stream

Photo Stream is turned off by default. To enable it on your iPhone you first need to make sure you have an iCloud account. See the box, *Signing up for iCloud*, on the opposite page to check that you have an iCloud account active on your iPhone. If you don't, you can set up a new one through the Mail, Contacts, Calendars entry in the iOS Settings application. When iCloud is up and running, tap Settings | iCloud, scroll down to the Photo Stream line, and then

Shared Photo Streams are a new feature in iOS 6 that let you share your photos with other users via Apple's servers.

Activating Photo Stream on your iPhone is a one-tap operation performed within the Setting app.

tap it to open its options. Tap each of the sliders beside My Photo Stream and Shared Photo Streams. We'll use Shared Photo Streams later on to make our images available to other users.

When you've finished, either step back up through the Settings menus or press the Home button to exit, then repeat the operation on each of your other iOS devices.

Photo Stream doesn't actually have an application of its own, as it is a service rather than an app. It therefore appears in other applications on your iPhone, including iPhoto, Pages and Keynote, as an album within the regular iOS photo store. The easiest way to find it is through the Photos app.

In iOS 6 this has been slightly re-designed with three icons at the bottom of the screen giving access to Albums, Photo Stream and Places. Tap Photo Stream to view your synchronised images.

The pictures that you see in this album are a collection gathered from each of your iOS devices. Some of them will have been taken using the iPhone on which you are viewing the Stream, but if you also have an iPad and iPod touch logged into the same account, their images will appear here, too. Photo Stream doesn't distinguish between the different devices used to shoot your photos here, so all of the images are organised in chronological order, with the most recent ones at the bottom of the list and the oldest, which will be the next ones to be removed if you exceed the 1000-shot or 30-day limit, at the top. You can see how many images reside in your photo stream at any time by checking the number in brackets beside the Photo Stream name. In the example shown below we have reached the prescribed limits, and so our images are being slowly erased from the Photo Stream.

Backing up your images

However, just because our images are disappearing from Photo Stream doesn't mean that we are losing them. Remember, Photo Stream is merely a synchronisation serice, not the primary store of your photographs.

Every image that you take will be retained on the device on which you originally shot it, even if it's removed from Photo Stream, so pictures that you take on your iPhone will stay there long after they disappear from your Stream. The same is true of images that you took with your iPad when they disappear from your iPhone, so you don't need to worry too much about

A minor redesign in iOS 6 has seen the tab for Photo Stream move to the bottom of the Photos app window.

The bracketed number beside your Photo Stream name is the number of images it contains. This Photo Stream contains 1000, so any new photos taken on this iPhone will cause the oldest to be removed.

what hitting this limit means. However, if you want to make sure that pictures you took at an event on your iPad remain available for use in Keynote presentations you put together on your iPhone you do need to take action while they're still in the Stream.

Copying your images from Photo Stream to the regular camera roll will move them onto your iPhone's internal storage, and from that point on they will be treated in exactly the same way as they would if they had been created on your iPhone in the first place. Follow the Technique guide below to copy your images from your Photo Stream to your iPhone, but bear in mind that lower-capacity phones will be able to store only a smaller number of images backed up this way.

Photo Stream on your Mac

Photo Stream also provides an easy way to back up your mobile photos on your Mac, but you need to have either Aperture or iPhoto installed on your machine to use it, and be running Mac OS X 10.7 or later.

Technique: Backing up your Photo Stream

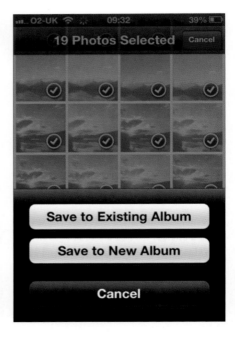

[1] Open your Photo Stream and tap Edit, then tap on each of the images you want to back up to apply a check mark.

[2] Tap Save at the bottom of the screen and choose whether to use a new or existing album. We're using a new one.

Before using either application you need to check that Photo Stream is enabled on your Mac through System Preferences. Click the iCloud pane and make sure that the box beside Photo Stream is ticked (see grab, right), then close System Preferences and launch iPhoto or Aperture.

[3] If creating a new album, give it a name. This must be unique, and not currently in use. Now tap Save.

[4] Your backed-up Photo Stream images are saved on your iPhone and are safe from automatic deletion.

If this is the first time you have run either since activating Photo Stream, it will detect the fact and ask whether you want to use it to synchronise your Mac with the images on your Stream. Click Turn on Photo Stream (see above). However, if you have already enabled either one of these apps to handle Photo Stream on your Mac for you and want to switch to the other, open the application Preferences pane (use the keyboard shortcut command-comma) and then check the box to use that application for Photo Stream (see below) and the other will be automatically disabled.

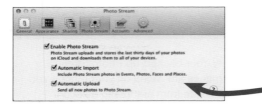

Turning on automatic import will draw down images sent to Photo Stream by your iOS devices, while automatic upload will send any photos added to iPhoto or Aperture back up to those same devices so that all remain in sync.

Opposite: Setting up Photo Stream on your Mac using iPhoto or Aperture will ensure that you always have a permanent backup copy of your library on your computer. Photos synchronised to either of these applications, or to folders on a Windows-based PC, won't be removed when you reach the 1000-image, 30-day limit on iCloud.

The synchronisation process works in both directions, so any photos you add to your iPhoto or Aperture libraries will also be synchronised back to your iOS devices in a shrunken-down form so that they don't consume too much room on your portable device and don't take too long to synchronise, particularly if you're working on a 3G connection. This allows you to use images you have shot using a regular compact camera or dSLR in your iPhone- or iPad-based creative projects.

Photo Stream on Windows

Windows users need to enable iCloud on their PCs by downloading the iCloud Control Panel from *icloud.com/ icloudcontrolpanel* after logging in using your regular credentials. (Note that it's not actually possible to create an iCloud account on a PC.)

Setting up Photo Stream on a Windows-based PC creates two folders, one of which handles downloads while the other takes care of images to be sent back up to iCloud and on from there to your iOS devices.

This small application adds an extra screen to the Windows Control Panel through which you can synchronise your data with that on Apple's servers.

The part that we're particularly interested in is the Photo Stream section, so check the box beside this and then click Options... to open a second panel. Here, you can specify which folders Windows should use to handle synchronisation with Apple's servers. The Control Panel will already have set up two folders for you inside your Pictures folder, but you can change these if you choose. The important point to note is that any images you drop in the Upload folder will appear on your iPhone, and any photos you take on your iPhone will automatically be sent to the Download folder.

Technique: Creating a shared Photo Stream

Shared Photo Streams are a brand new feature in iOS 6 that let you share your images with other users through a regular web browser, without having to use a feature like Journals in iPhoto.

You have to enable this feature through Settings | iCloud | Photo Stream, as shared Photo Streams are not activated by default. When you have switched it on, follow the Technique steps below to share.

[1] Open the album containing the photos that you want to share. They don't need to be contained in their own dedicated album, so start by looking in your regular Camera Roll. When you have created the Shared Stream you'll be able to find them more easily as they'll be given a dedicated folder. Tap on each of the photos you want to share and you'll see that it is greyed out and overlaid by a tick.

[2] Now tap the Share button at the bottom of the screen to call up the regular iOS sharing pane. If you only want to send your photos to one person, consider using Message. To publish them, though, tap Photo Stream.

[3] Every Photo Stream needs a name, so choose one now, making sure that it is unique, and enter the contact details of the person who will be able to see

the images. Now write a short covering note to the person with whom you are sharing your photos. They will receive this as an email.

[4] Your new Photo Stream will be created, and the person with whom you have shared it will receive an email containing a direct link to your photos. You can delete your shared Photo Stream though the Photo Stream tab.

Chapter 4
Sharing your photos

Share your photos over email

Email is one of the simplest ways to share your photos. The iPhone has a first class built-in client, which means that you don't even need to synchronise them to your Mac or PC before sending them to friends and family. You'd need to have a very good reason not to make this your primary means of sharing images on a one-to-one or one-to-few basis, particularly if you don't need an immediate response.

There are two ways in which you can email photos using the native tools rather than any third-party clients. The first is to start in the Photos application and select the photos you want to send from your Camera Roll, Albums or Photo Stream and then use the regular sharing shortcut to dispatch them. This is by far the simplest method, and since the arrival of iOS 6 it's been possible to send more than one image at a time by selecting several in a sequence, which is a big productivity timesaver.

The second method is to start in the Mail application, write the body of your message and then copy and paste the image into it. This is a little more fiddly, though, as it requires some switching backwards and forwards. Previously it was the only way that you could send more than one image at a time using Apple's own email client.

Whichever method you choose, you'll have to specify what image size you want to use. iOS asks you this as smaller images consume less space, so will be sent more quickly and won't hammer your monthly data cap quite so heavily if you're not on wifi. Only use large images when quality is paramount.

Reducing the size of the embedded images in your messages is a good way to reduce your bandwidth consumption and avoid using up too much of your monthly data plan limit

Technique: Sharing photos over email

Method 1: From the Photos app

[1] Open the Photos app and navigate to the album or photo stream containing the images you want to send.

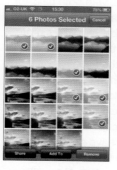

[2] Tap Edit and then select each of the images you want to send. If you want to send them by email, select five or fewer or the email option disappears.

[3] Tap the Share button and then select Mail as the sharing method. Your images will be dropped into a new message in the email client.

Method 2: From the email client

[1] Open the email client, start a new message and type out the recipient address and the body of your email.

[2] Switch to the Photos app, open the album containing your image and locate it, then hold your finger on the photo until Copy appears. Tap the Copy bubble.

[3] Return to your message and hold down your finger on a blank space in your email until the menu pops up. Tap the Paste button.

Sharing your photos on Flickr

Owned and run by Yahoo, Flickr is probably the web's easiest tool for sharing your photos with friends, family and the public at large. No wonder it has built itself such a loyal following among both hobby and professional photographers.

You don't get much control over the look of your Flickr photostream, but the payoff is that you don't have to spend any time thinking about design or coding, either. All you do is upload your photos, apply the relevant tags, and, if you want, write a few captions.

More and more services are seeing the value of Flickr and using it either as a source from which to draw in pictures for use in other projects, or to which

they post images for online use. Where the iPhone is concerned, we're most interested in the second option, but that doesn't mean that the first is irrelevant. Uploading your images to Flickr direct from your iPhone means you can then go on to use them in other products either on your Mac or PC without either using Photo Stream or transferring them by email from your handset.

Signing up for Flickr

There are two different account types open to Flickr users, with both paid-for and free options. Naturally, the paid-for option is more flexible and offers more features. However, that's not to say there's no value in the freebie.

To get started, point your browser at flickr.com and click Sign Up at the top of the page. Flickr lets you sign in with an existing Facebook or Google account, but if you have neither of these you can create a new account from scratch by signing up for a Yahoo ID. You'll need to supply your name, date of birth and other personal details, select a login ID and password, and provide the answers to some standard questions that it can use to verify who you are if you forget your password.

The free account lets you upload a maximum of 300MB worth of images each month, with a limit on each image size of 30MB. Your 200 most recent

Photostream vs Photo Stream

Confused by the difference between these seemingly quite similar terms? Photo Stream, with a space between the two words, is the phrase used by Apple to describe the synchronised set of images that is managed between your iOS devices via iCloud.

Photostream, without a space, is the term Flickr has long used to describe the stream of images you have uploaded to your account and made availabe online.

They are incompatible technologies and can't share each others' data.

	Flickr Free account	Flickr Pro account
Maximum monthly uploads	300MB	Unlimited
Maximum single image size	30MB	50MB
Maximum images in stream	200	Unlimited
Maximum number of groups	10	60
Download options	Smaller, resized images	Original images
Monthly video upload limit	2 per month, up to 150MB each	Unlimited, up to 500MB each
Other benefits	None	No adverts on site Bundled account stats
Ongoing costs	Free	$6.95 per quarter $24.95 per year $44.95 for two years

photos will be visible on the site and you can organise them into 10 groups. You can upload up to two videos a month and download smaller, resized versions of your original photos if you happen to lose your master copies.

Upgrading to a Flickr Pro account gives you more flexibility. You can upload as many images as you want and the file size limit is raised to 50MB per photo. All of your images will be visible in your library, not just the most recent 200, and you can organise them into as many as 60 different groups. If you lose your originals you can download high resolution versions of each one at the same size as those lost original files, and you can upload and play as many high definition videos as you want. You can also track how many people are looking at your photos over time with the bundled stats and use the site without any ads getting in the way.

Flickr is one of the web's most popular photo sharing sites, used by amateurs and professionals alike. Even the free account terms are fairly generous.

Flickr has paid plans for three months, one year and two year memberships depending on how long you want to commit to the site, but it makes sense in the first instance to stick with the free account to see whether it suits your needs and upgrade to Pro if you're sure that Flickr is right for you.

Right now, you won't have any photos on your Flickr photo stream, so there's nothing for anyone to see on your account. Before you start uploading images, though, it's worth taking a little time to write a profile that people will see when they visit your Photostream. This helps them to put your photos in context.

Flickr provides all the tools you need to maintain very fine-grained control over your privacy settings so that you can specify who can find you in search results and what others can do with your images. You need never divulge more info than you're comfortable with.

Flickr for iPhone

If you prefer to use a native client for uploading your images to Flickr, there are plenty to choose from in the App Store. For the best support, though, check out the official Flickr for iPhone application by pointing your browser at http://itunes.apple.com/us/app/flickr/id328407587

Click your username at the top of the screen and then, on the personal information tab that appears, click Edit on the line beside Your Profile.

Use the various boxes to write a little bit about yourself, promote your own website and help people get in touch either by email or instant messenger. Be careful not to give away too much personal information, though, or anything that can put your safety at risk.

While you're tweaking your account this way it is also worth taking time to have a think about your privacy. Flickr makes it very easy to specify how your information should be used and where it should be visible.

Once you have saved your profile, click the Privacy & Permissions tab within the Your Account area and work your way through at least the Global Settings section specifying how people can find you, what they can do with your

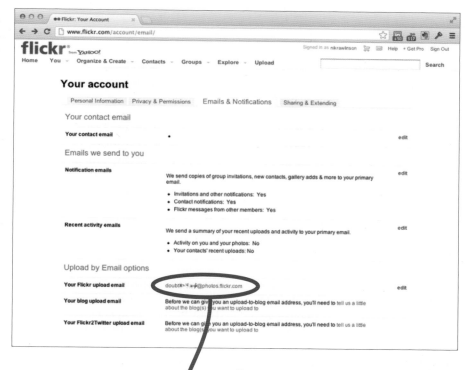

You can upload images to Flickr without using a client app by emailing them to the unique upload email address associated with your account.

images and whether or not your profile and photos should appear in public searches.

The more of these options you shut down, the less of your information will be spread about, but at the same time you lower your chances of being found, which makes Flickr a less effective channel through which to promote your photography. As ever, it's a matter of being sensible and carefully balancing the costs and benefits of each approach.

Uploading images

Although the most recent releases of Apple's desktop and laptop operating system, OS X, have Flickr integration at the core, and allow you to upload images directly from the default applications, such tight integration isn't yet a feature of iOS on the iPhone.

Fortunately there are plenty of third-party upload tools that can plug the gap if you'd rather use an application tied in to the service to manage your uploads.

However, if you'd prefer not to add any new applications to an already busy set of home screens, you can upload just as easily using the built-in email client.

Open your Flickr account pages (click your username at the top of the screen) and click Emails & Notifications (see the screen grab on the previous page).

Scroll down this page until you reach the Upload by Email options section and make a note of the address beside Your Flickr upload email.

This address is unique to your account and shouldn't be shared with anyone else, as it would allow them to send images to your Flickr photostream Add it to your address book under a logical contact name, such as Flickr Upload, so that you don't need to remember it.

Now, when you want to send an image to your Flickr Photostream, open it in the iPhone Photos app and tap the sharing button, followed by Mail.

The image will be attached to a new message in the usual manner; all you need to do is select your unique upload address from the contacts list and tap Send to dispatch it to Flickr.

The technique described above will add your image to your Photostream and make it available in line with your site-wide privacy settings. However, with a little bit of tweaking you can make it a whole lot more flexible, still without downloading a dedicated uploader app.

Emailed uploads and photo privacy

Although you can set a general site-wide series of privacy controls, you can also set them on an image-by-image basis when uploading your photo by tweaking the email address.

Let's imagine that your email address is the same as the one we showed in the image on the previous page – doubt******@photos.flickr.com

Adding the names of groups before the @ symbol means that only those people who appear in those groups will be able to see your image. So, doubt******+family@photos.flickr.com would restrict visibility of the uploaded image to just family members. For any image you want to keep private, so that only you can access it, you'd swap the +family for +private, and you'd use +public to make it visible to everyone.

There are five default levels of privacy that you can apply to your images in this way, and it makes sense to save a Contacts list entry for each one so that you don't have to type them all in.

Email privacy settings

+family . . . . visible to family only
+friends . . . . .visible to friends only
+ff . . . . .visible to friends and family
+private . . . . .only visible to yourself
+public . . . . visible to everyone

Filing your photos by email

Uploading your photos this way, even if you add elements to the address that make them more or less visible than your default account settings permit, doesn't do much to help keep them organised in your Photostream. Fortunately, by adding some extra details to the subject line or body of the enclosing email you can do this remotely without having to log in and make changes directly through the site. The secret lies in careful use of the message body and subject line.

The subject line is where you enter your image title. The title appears immediately below the image when displayed in your Photostream and will be the most obvious clue that your visitors get to the subject matter (if your picture is a landscape or scenic shot, the fact that iPhone images are location-tagged using the internal GPS chip means visitors will also be able to see what it depicts by clicking on the map beside the image).

Use the message body to enter a short descriptive passage that will appear below the heading (see above), and then if you want to provide any tags under which the picture will be filed, add these on a new line below that. It's important that the tags appear on their own line, without any other content beside them, and that each one is separated by a comma that deliniates where one stops and the next begins.

Location-stamping images

To enable location stamping of your images, open Settings | Privacy | Location Services, tap the slider to turn on Location Services and make sure the slider beside Camera is set to ON.

Sharing your photos on Facebook

Facebook was a latecomer to iOS, finally arriving in iOS 6 (Twitter beat it by appearing at the same time as iOS 5).

Sharing to Facebook works in a very similar way to sharing with Twitter, except that rather than posting to a general forum to which everyone with a browser has access, the Facebook posting feature sends images to your Wall, which means you can control who has access to them, and even keep them entirely private so that nobody can see them but you.

Technique: Photos on Facebook

The iOS Facebook feature lets you post direct from a variety of built-in apps and, because it can interrogate your account for your pre-defined groups, lets you keep your posts private.

[1] The easiest way to send a quick update to Facebook without opening a Facebook client is to pull down on the clock to open Notification Center and then tap in the Tap to Post box close to the top.

[2] However, we are interested in posting images, so we've switched to the Photos app and tapped the share button on the bottom toolbar. This calls up the ways in which you can share your content with friends, at the centre of which is the Facebook option. Tap this.

[3] This calls up the Facebook posting card with the photo that we want to post to our account clipped to it. Here we are write a description so that it makes sense when it appears on our account, as it's not immediately obvious what the image depicts. We can geo-locate it by tapping the Add Location link below it and tap Post to send it.

[4] Facebook lets you organise your contacts into groups, and you can make your post visible to just a small selection by tapping Friends in the lower right corner of the card and selecting a group.

Share your photos on Twitter

Twitter has been built in to iOS since version 5. Along with Facebook, it's one of the world's most widely-used social networks, and a very effective route through which to share your images with friends, family and colleagues.

You need a Twitter account before you share your images this way, so either point your browser at *twitter. com* and sign up there, or on your iPhone tap through to Settings | Twitter | Add Account and tap the Create New Account button.

Technique: Tweet your photos

Once you've set up your Twitter account, you've done all you need to start sharing your photos using the four simple steps outlined below.

[1] Navigate to the album or photo stream containing the images you want to share and tap the Edit button at the top of the interface. Tap on the image you want to send to Twitter, bearing in mind that unlike Email, which lets you share a maximum of five images at a

time, Twitter only lets you post one in each tweet when using the iOS tools.

[2] Tap the Share button and then select Twitter as the sharing method.

[3] Your photo will be clipped to a new message card on which you can type a covering note to be posted alongside the image. Although you can write up to 140 characters on a plain tweet you won't be able to write that many here as

a few characters will be consumed by the link to the image.

[4] If you are tweeting a photo of a particular location, sharing the place from which you're tweeting (taking care not to reveal enough to put your personal safety at risk) can help people understand where it it. Tap Add Location if you want to do this, and then decide whether or not all devices should have the right to tweet your position.

Chapter 5

Accessories

Studio Neat Glif and Glif+

Nobody can deny that the iPhone is a truly beautiful piece of kit. Its sleek front and back, and its thin form factor, make it a true object of desire, whichever version you have. But... they don't exactly make it easy to hold when you're taking a picture, and if you need to balance your iPhone on a ledge so that you can take a shot hands-free, things get decidedly tricky indeed.

That's where Glif comes to the rescue. This neat plastic cradle slips onto the edge and corner of an iPhone and provides a regular quarter-inch screw thread by which you can attach it to a regular tripod.

If you upgrade to the Glif+ package then not only do you get the tripod mount, but you also get Serif, which reaches around the back of the iPhone to provide a second vertical support, and Ligature, which is a quarter-inch screw that fixes into the tripod screw hole to attach Glif and Serif (which itself fits inside Glif) to your keychain, so wherever you're shooting with your iPhone you'll always have your kit close at hand.

The Glif+ bundle comes packaged in a neat cardboard box with chiselled edges that makes a handy stand when fixed together using the Ligature, which means you don't even need to have a tripod to keep your iPhone upright.

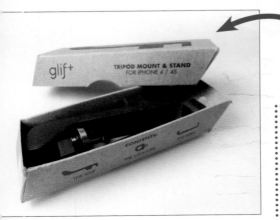

The Glif+ bundle includes Serif, a clever second brace to hold your iPhone secure, and Ligature, a quarter-inch screw that both helps you keep it on your keychain.

The Skinny

Glif and Glif+ are both available from *studioneat.com* for international delivery and can be bought through Amazon. They work with iPhone 4, 4S and 5

Olloclip

Olloclip is three lenses in one smart clip-on unit that hugs the corner of your iPhone. One lens is fish eye lens, which gives you approximately 180 degrees of coverage of your surroundings. Flipping it around so that the opposite lens is in front of the iPhone camera gives you a macro lens with around 10x magnification and which, when unscrewed, exposes the third lens, which caters for regular wide angle photography.

It's extremely well made and comes with its own tidy carrying bag so you can slip it into your pocket without worrying too much about it being damaged. Each lens has a cap to protect it when not in use.

Not only does Olloclip's fish eye lens give you a wider angle of view, but as you can see from the shots below we also found that it resulted in far punchier blue skies.

The fisheye lens gives you almost a 180-degree view, turning flat scenes like this into something special.

Before

After

The Skinny

For more details and a gallery of images, point your browser at *olloclip.com*. The current version works with iPhone 4 and 4S, but an iPhone 5 version is in the works.

Apple stalk with 10x magnification

The Olloclip macro lens, which sits in front of the wide angle glass, delivers magnification equivalent to around 10x

Thumbs Up Fisheye lens

The Fisheye Lens screws into a thread in a bundled iPhone case, which keeps it aligned with the iPhone's built-in camera lens

If you don't need all of the lenses that come bundled up in the Olliclip, check out this stand-alone fisheye lens. It offers an angle of view of approximately 160 degrees, helping you to cram more into each shot and save you the chore of stitching together a panorama.

There are various versions for different designs of iPhone, and rather than slipping onto the corner of the phone as the Olliclip does they come with a bundled case that has a clever screw thread to position the lens right in front of the iPhone's built-in camera.

The Skinny

Find further details online at *thumbsupuk.com.* The lens is available for the iPhone 3G, 3GS, 4 and 4S.

Before

After

iPhone Microscope

The iPhone's built-in camera is already pretty good at doing close-up photos, particularly with later versions now boasting a nice wide aperture to ensure a pleasingly shallow depth of field.

With a microscope, though, you can take things even further. This particular example magnifies at between 60x and 100x, depending on how far you have turned the zoom control on the underside. The only other control is a focus wheel, which you'll need to use to trim the clarity of the result as you change the level of magnification.

Obviously, putting a lens that close to your subject could lead to you blocking out some of the available light with your hand, so the iPhone Microscope also has a built-in light, which you can switch on using a small switch at the side. It's slightly blue, but the iPhone seems to cope with compensating for this in the results.

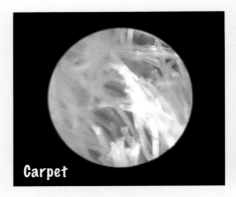

Carpet

We did find working with the iPhone Microscope to be a little tricky at first, and it required a bit of hit-and-miss trial-and-error to get it right. We also found that some subjects gave better results than others, so it's worth picking and choosing what you work with carefully.

The lens itself is fairly large, so as with others seen here it attaches to your iPhone using a bundled case.

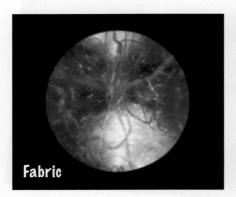

Fabric

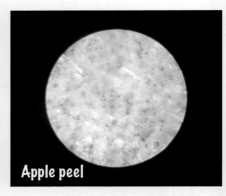

Apple peel

The built-in lamp keeps your subject illuminated when you're doing close-up work so that the iPhone and your hands don't block out the available light

Wooden table

The Skinny

The Microscope works with iPhone 4. Find further details online at *thumbsupuk.com*

Telephoto Lens for iPhone

Apart from the various buttons and switches, the iPhone has no moving parts. That means you can't physically zoom in on your subject, and the only zooming you can do is digital, by unpinching your fingers on the screen to stretch your subject. This is effective if you don't take things too far, but as all you're actually doing is enlarging the central portion you risk degrading the result if you don't take care.

The Telephoto Lens for iPhone goes some way to fixing that problem by giving you a fixed 12x zoom when it's positioned in front of the camera aperture by screwing it into the thread on the bundled iPhone case.

It's not particularly heavy, but it's made of glass and metal, rather than plastic, and so comes with a bundled tripod to keep it steady. This can attach directly to the lens itself using a screw on the cuff that surrounds the narrower end of the barrel, or into a clamp that ships with the bundled case and

These two shots were taken from the same position. The one on the right was taken with the Telephoto Lens.

surrounds the screen side of your phone.

Overall build quality is excellent and the level of magnification is impressive. It doesn't take up much room in a pocket or back and, when used with care, it can make a big difference to your shots and produce enormously magnified subjects.

The Skinny

The Telephoto Lens is available for iPhone 4. Find further details online at *vtec.co.uk*

Eye Scope

The Eyescope magnifies what your iPhone camera can see by 8x to get you closer to you subject either when you can't move from your current position, or the subject is small or impractical.

It's made from plastic, rather than metal, but is nonetheless very well built. There's a manual focus ring at the front, which has been coated in rubber to make it easier to grip. The action is very smooth and it makes a significant difference to the quality of your results.

As with the Telephoto Lens for iPhone it's bundled with both an iPhone case into which the narrow end screws to line it up with the camera lens, and a small tripod to help you hold it still.

However, it also ships with an elasticated clamp that grips the iPhone top and bottom and provides the mount point for the tripod (you can also screw in a regular tripod as it uses a standard quarter-inch screw aperture).

Although you obviously don't get the same magnification as you do with the Telephoto Lens for iPhone, 8x is nonetheless an impressive metric and by stepping down slightly you save some space in your pocket with this smaller, lighter lens.

With 8x magnification, the Eyescope lets you get closer to your subject without changing position.

The Eyescope is a screw-in telescope for the iPhone offering 8x magnification in a lightweight plastic body

The Skinny

Find further details of Eyescope, which is available for iPhone 4, and where to buy at *thumbsupuk.com*

At the front of the lens barrel there's a rubber-coated focus ring that lets you adjust image sharpness

Glossary

Bluetooth Short-range radio networking standard, allowing compatible devices to 'see' and interrogate each other to discover their shared abilities and then use these abilities to swap information. It is commonly used to connect mobile phones and headsets for hands-free calling, but is also seen on keyboards and mice used with desktop computers. Where photography is concerned, iPhoto for iPhone and iPad uses Bluetooth to wirelessly 'beam' images to other iPhoto users.

Compression When images on a website or music on an iPhone or iPod are made smaller so that they either download more quickly or take up less space in the device's memory they are said to have been compressed. Compression involves selectively removing parts of the file that are less easily seen or heard by the human eye and ear and simplifying the more complex parts. The most common use of compression in photography involved removing changes in colour from an image in places where the human eye wouldn't notice that they were missing. This enables the device, such as an iPhone, to reduce the size of an image before sharing it or publishing it online, or simply to reduce the amount of space that it consumes on its internal storage. Applying too much compression will degrade the quality of the image.

Dock Cradle designed for use with an iPhone or iPod that supports the device while it is charging and transfers data to and from a host computer using a bundled connector.

Encoding The process of capturing an analogue data source, such as a sound or an image, and translating it into a digital format. Although files can be encoded with no loss of quality, the process usually also involves compression to reduce the resulting file sizes. Where photography is concerned, the encoding involves translating the analogue light measurements coming in through the lens into a digital data stream.

GB / Gigabyte One billion bytes, and a means of measuring the capacity of a device. A byte is made up of eight bits, and a bit is equivalent to a single character, such as a, b, c, 4, 5, 6 and so on. As digital images are encoded using the characters 0 and 1, each digit that makes up part of its encoding will represent one bit, every eight characters will make one byte, every 1,024 bytes will equal a kilobyte and every billion bytes will equate to a gigabyte. To put this into context, the iPhone has a capacity of up to 32GB. If this was devoted entirely to music, then, by Apple's calculations for the equivalent 32GB iPod touch, it would be able to hold about 7,000 songs at iTunes' default settings. As an iPhone photo takes up much less space than this – typically less than a megabyte – you can store many thousands of images on even the lowest capacity phone at any one time before you need to start thinking about streamlining your library.

Home Screen As used within this book, the term used to describe the screen within the iPhone's interface that displays the icons for the installed applications

iCloud Online synchronisation service owned and run by Apple from several data centres around the world. Provides backup services for iPhones, iPads, iPod touches and other Apple hardware, and shares both documents and images. Most importantly where photography is concerned, it is the backbone of the company's Photo Stream synchronisation service.

iPad Portable computer device invented and sold by Apple. It uses the same operating system as the iPhone and can run compatible applications, but boasts a larger screen, making it easier to type on than the iPhone or iPod touch. Does not have phone features, but connects to the Internet by means of wifi or a 3G cellphone network connection. It has a lower-resolution camera than iPhone.

Megapixel One million pixels. A measurement used to quantify the ability of a digital camera to capture information. The higher the megapixel measurement, the more information it will capture, leading to larger file sizes, but allowing for the captured image to be either printed on a larger scale or cropped to highlight smaller details. It is a common misconception that higher megapixel counts lead to sharper images, which is not always the case, as image crispness often depends as much on the quality of the lens in front of the sensor and the relative size, rather than resolution, of the sensor itself.

MobileMe Online service run by Apple to provide a range of features of use to Mac owners, including email, online storage, calendar synchronisation across multiple machines and basic backup tools. Following criticism of the integrated features and level of service, it was given a significant upgrade in summer 2007 and a new look in 2009. It was retired in 2011, when iCloud took over many of its functions.

OS X Operating system developed by Apple, a variant of which is used inside the iPhone and later versions of the iPod under the name iOS. It shares a common core with Apple's modern operating system for laptop and desktop computers, Mac OS X, which was developed from code it inherited when it acquired Steve Jobs' NeXT computer company. The X in its name is pronounced 'ten' since it is the tenth major iteration of the operating system.

Photo Stream Service that forms part of iCloud, which synchronises the 1000 most recent photos you have taken on an iPhone, iPod touch or iPad over the last 30 days with each of your other devices logged in to the same account. After 30 days, or when you have shot more than 1000 photos, the oldest items start to be removed from synchronised devices to make room for new content to be added.

SMS Short Message Service. Commonly referred to as text messages, SMS is a means of sending brief notes between mobile handsets, which was initially developed as a means for network operators to send messages to their subscribers. SMS messages are generally restricted to 160 characters or fewer, although many phones – including the iPhone – can thread together multiple discrete messages to make a single, longer communication. SMS is handled on the iPhone by the Messages application, through which it allows you to share your images with other phone users, and iPad, iPod touch, iPhone and Mac users of other Messages clients.

Sync Short for synchronise. The means of swapping data between the iPhone and a desktop or laptop computer so that the information on each – including music, photos, contacts and so on – mirrors the other. Traditionally performed by connecting the two using the bundled Dock connector cable, although Apple is now enabling wireless synchronisation on a local wifi network for those devices running iOS 5 or later.

Toolbar Any area within a piece of software that houses buttons to perform common functions. On the iPhone, most system-based toolbars, such as those found in Safari, run along the bottom of the screen, while navigation buttons generally appear at the top. This is an unwritten rule, however, and many applications – both from Apple and third-party developers – are increasingly putting controls at the top of the application Window. Pages, for example, clusters many of its formatting tools on a strip at the top of the screen.

USB Universal Serial Bus. A socket, plug and cable system that allows almost any peripheral to be connected to a Mac or PC, including printers, mice, keyboards and so on. The iPhone and iPod also use USB as a means of exchanging data with a computer and, as the cable can carry power, charging their batteries.